Forgotten FAITH

AWAKENING A HOPE WE NO LONGER KNOW

Forgotten FAITH

AWAKENING A HOPE WE NO LONGER KNOW

LAUREN REEVES

© 2019 by Lauren Reeves. All rights reserved.

Published by Redemption Press, PO Box 427, Enumclaw, WA 98022.

Toll-Free (844) 2REDEEM (273-3336)

Redemption Press is honored to present this title in partnership with the author. The views expressed or implied in this work are those of the author. Redemption Press provides our imprint seal representing design excellence, creative content, and high-quality production.

No part of this publication may be reproduced, stored in a retrieval system, or transmitted in any way by any means—electronic, mechanical, photocopy, recording, or otherwise—without the prior permission of the copyright holder, except as provided by USA copyright law.

All Scripture quotations, unless otherwise indicated, are taken from the Holy Bible, English Standard Version. ESV® Permanent Text Edition® (2016). Copyright © 2001 by Crossway Bibles, a publishing ministry of Good News Publishers.

Scripture quotations marked NASB are taken from the New American Standard Bible® (NASB), Copyright © 1960, 1962, 1963, 1968, 1971, 1972, 1973, 1975, 1977, 1995 by The Lockman Foundation. Used by permission. www.Lockman.org

Scripture quotations marked NIV are taken from the Holy Bible, New International Version®, NIV® Copyright ©1973, 1978, 1984, 2011 by Biblica, Inc.® Used by permission. All rights reserved worldwide.

Scripture quotations marked NLT are taken from the Holy Bible, New Living Translation, copyright © 1996, 2004, 2015 by Tyndale House Foundation. Used by permission of Tyndale House Publishers Inc., Carol Stream, Illinois 60188. All rights reserved.

Scripture quotations marked KJV are taken from the Holy Bible, King James Version, © 1979, 1980, 1982 by Thomas Nelson, Inc., Publishers. Used by permission.

Scripture quotations marked NKJV are taken from the New King James Version. Copyright © 1982 by Thomas Nelson, Inc. Used by permission. All rights reserved.

ISBN 13: 978-1-68314-950-7 (Paperback)
978-1-68314-951-4 (ePub)
978-1-68314-952-1 (Mobi)

Library of Congress Catalog Card Number: 2019915396

For Granny—
Your life has always laid the path of faith before me,
and now the heartache of your death reminds me I'm not home.
I love you and will see you when I get there . . .

Table of Contents

Introduction...ix
Chapter 1:   The Master Designer (Creation).................. 11
Chapter 2:   Undo Button (Adam & Eve)........................ 21
Chapter 3:   Worthiness (Cain & Abel) 37
Chapter 4:   The End Times (Enoch, Methuselah & Noah) 49
Chapter 5:   A Tale of Two Cities (Nimrod's Tower of Babel) . 69
Chapter 6:   Everlasting Promises (Abraham).................. 87
Chapter 7:   Two Types of Believers (Abraham & Lot)......... 103
Chapter 8:   The Waging War (Isaac vs. Ishmael; Jacob vs. Esau)...... 119
Chapter 9:   Great Lengths (Jacob) 137
Chapter 10: Not Forgotten (Jacob & the Twelve Tribes of Israel) 151
Chapter 11: Unveiling the End (Joseph)..................... 177
Final Word from the Author.................................. 189
Endnotes 193
Bibliography.. 199

Introduction

CHRISTIAN AUTHOR AND SPEAKER Voddie Baucham once said, "The modern church is producing passionate people with empty heads who love the Jesus they don't know very well."[1] When believers are challenged to explain what they believe and why, too many fall short. We are a passionate people, but do the majority of Christians really know what they believe? Do we know how Christianity got here? Are we able to maintain hope in the midst of pain, loss, and heartache because we truly understand the promises and end plan God has laid out for us? I pray this book will take you into a deeper understanding of the beliefs we claim so we can each endure and unshakably stand firm to the end.

I've often been told that Genesis is foundational in understanding the rest of the Bible. Within these pages you'll find a fascinating study of Genesis, but you will also find that the first book of Genesis and the last book of Revelation in the Bible go hand in hand as a good opening and closing often do. In this book, you will glean the lessons God laid out in Genesis to be warning, prophecy, and hope in a future that is surer than anything we can know. Additionally, I truly believe the concepts explained on these pages will allow you to read and understand the rest of Scripture in a new and fresh way.

What we will find as we journey through Genesis together is that the Bible was inspired even from its very first words. The Master Planner had the end already mapped out from the beginning. I'm excited to accompany you on this journey. May the blessing of God rest on us as we study Genesis together.

This book has been soaked in tears and prayers as I begged God to glorify Himself through the pages. While I was working on this book, there were days where I felt like the persistent widow who kept knocking and knocking, except I wasn't knocking on a literal door, I was knocking on heaven's door in prayer for you and for me. He may allow me through the Holy Spirit to deposit the seeds of truth onto pages of a book, but I have learned it is He who waters and grows them. He has designed us to be dependent on Him, so He allows for no gift great enough in any of us to water and grow our own seeds. We always plead to Him for that. So, know I have plead at heaven's door for you and for me with many tears.

May He bring forth fruit in abundance in our lives through His Holy Spirit, and may we always seek and trust His promises to one day make all things new (Rev. 21:5). Let's journey together to make Christianity's *Forgotten Faith* become a faith that is remembered, strong, firm, and contagious.

CHAPTER 1

The Master Designer
(Creation)

I LIKE TO CREATE. I like writing songs and poetry, bringing them into existence from the emotions stirring inside. I like to take a blank canvas of a house and paint and design and decorate it into something beautiful. I like to see a person, not only for who they are, but for what they could be with the hope and work of God. I like to find animals with issues that might cause them to end up dumped on the street, and create a life for them better than they ever could have hoped for otherwise. To help make something out of nothing is woven into me by the heart of my Maker because that's how He is. The difference is I have to use what's already created to create something beautiful because I can't actually create something out of nothing. My mind and heart are already created, which I use to usher words into songs and poetic journal entries. I see an already created house or person or animal and see them for what they could become with a little shelter, food, love, or effort.

A builder uses already created materials, and pharmacists and scientists use chemicals found in already created plants and animals to create medicines. Ecclesiastes is correct when it says there is nothing new under the sun. We can reorganize, re-beautify, or restructure, but in every instance, we start with something already created. We start with some piece of matter that has been created and is already here.

God is the only one who can truly make something out of absolutely nothing. That's what scholars mean by the phrase *creation ex nihilo*. That phrase literally means "creation out of nothing." God is outside of the natural laws of the world we know. He is outside of time and space, which makes Him able to create and rule everything we know inside time and space with a better perspective. The very first verses of the Bible speak of when God created the heavens and the earth. "In the beginning, God created the heavens and the earth. The earth was without form and void, and darkness was over the face of the deep. And the Spirit of God was hovering over the face of the waters" (Gen. 1:1–2). Take note of the part of the verse that says, "The earth was without form and void, and darkness was over the face of the deep." Darkness is the *absence* of light. The earth was without form and void. There was truly nothing. And then God started speaking things into existence, creating something out of nothing. And not just a little something, but something grand and gorgeous and breathtaking.

The question of creation is a debated one. Scripture has been brought into question by some because the Bible seems to infer that the date of creation is about six thousand years ago, while scientists date the earth to be billions of years old. Sure, the scientist's dating methods and tools could be wrong, and some have proven to be wrong (e.g., carbon dating), but how do we reconcile such a stark difference in age theories? Did God speak into existence an already aged universe? Is that why it seems from the text that God created Adam as an already physically mature man rather than a baby? Or were there simply spans of time that were unspecified between verses? There are possible interpretations that can reconcile the Bible's dating with scientific dating if we find one day that the scientific dating methods are one hundred percent accurate. The idea of God creating an already aged universe is just one theory to consider.

But it is an interesting one because we know that Jesus was able to instantly age matter by looking at his very first miracle at Cana when He turned water into wine (John 2:1–11)—and not just any wine—wine that was described as the best wine. The best wine is well-aged wine. Jesus turned water into wine and aged it instantly as His very first miracle on earth. Could this be a glimpse of what He did for us at the very beginning of the world? If so, it was probably a greater mercy than we know. Today, compost piles are made by humans, using the process of decay over time in order to put richer nutrients into the ground to make better soil for plants. It could be that God aged the environment in His own miraculous way in order to get it ready for the initial humans, plants, and animals to thrive. Or maybe there were spans of time between certain acts of creation that Scripture does not implicitly reveal. It's possible the "days of creation" in Genesis were symbolic of spans of time rather than literal twenty-four-hour days. We cannot know for sure.

Another popular notion about how the world began is the Big Bang Theory. I'm sure you've heard of it. The very simplified version of this theory is the concept that our universe exploded into being—randomly from particles. Scientists have found indications pointing to an event like this, so some of them use these findings to try to disprove the Bible's explanation of creation. But actually, a universe that started with a big bang can support Scripture's creation account. Physicists and scientists who try to counter the Bible might say the Big Bang happened randomly by chance, but if God spoke things into being by saying, "Let there be," couldn't His spoken creation of something out of nothing cause a sort of event that would be seen thousands or billions of years later as a Big Bang event?

Evolution is another "how we got here" theory that keeps people from believing the Bible and Christianity. There are some Christian theologians that embrace evolution and have ways of interpreting the Bible to allow for this theory, but I have problems with it at this point. Evolutionists teach a progression stating humans evolved from apes and therefore challenge the literal creation account of the Bible. The theory of evolution, though, isn't just a progression teaching that humans came from apes. The progression of evolution actually starts from a warm water dwelling amoeba. The amoeba evolves in its warm pond into some sort of fish, which evolves into a lizard, which evolves into an animal of some type, which evolves into an ape, and then a human. Now, they don't adequately explain what created the original warm pond or the very first amoeba with surprisingly complex DNA, but that's apparently beside the point.

The point I'm trying to make here is their evidence has *major* missing links between species that, if they could be discovered, might help prove evolution. But contrary to what some fake news articles say, the proof is *not* there to prove the transition between apes and humans. I've noticed a lot of people like to point out that the DNA makeup of the closest species of ape is around 90% the same as humans. And when I first heard this, I'll admit I was a little more interested. But then I found out some studies are finding mice have a DNA makeup that is around 90% the same as humans too. Apparently the remaining 5–10% difference makes a big impact. (For great information on evolution and other tough topics, read *I Don't Have Enough Faith to Be an Atheist* by Normal L. Geisler and Frank Turek.)

So, yes, similarities are present between species, but big inferences are being made to explain those similarities. I do believe that God created humans as well as other species with the ability to adapt and change as needed over time, but it is too big of an assumption to say humans came from apes just because there are similarities. Shouldn't we *expect* some similarities within a creation designed by the same Creator and Artist?

I used to collect Precious Moments figurines. They were designed by a man named Samuel John Butcher. No matter if the character molded into a figurine was a dog, cat, human, or any other species, they each had the mark of the artist's style. The figurines were known for their teardrop style eyes as well as soft colors and smooth shape. In the same way we can know a Vincent van Gogh painting as being painted by van Gogh or a Leonardo da Vinci painting as being by da Vinci simply because of the unique touch of the artist. Shouldn't it be the same with the Master Artist? Couldn't it be appropriate of Him to use similar internal organ structure in several species even though they are not directly related to one another? Couldn't it be right of Him to use similar body structure in two different species without allowing them to be directly related, but rather, different and unique to one another?

The fields of science and religion do not have to be in opposition. The field of religion has mistakenly drawn the wrong inferences from Scripture at times in the past, just as the field of science has mistakenly drawn the wrong inferences from what could be seen, heard, touched, and tasted. Scientists and physicists give themselves room for error by calling their inferences "theories." Theories aren't facts. They are guesses based on what humans have the capacity to see. Guesses are fine and are often necessary to move forward in exploration. Theories only become dangerous to the soul of a human when they begin to be taught as if they were proven facts. I believe when Scripture and matter are interpreted correctly, religion and science can walk hand in hand, each helping the other to see clearly.

Regardless of which of the many theories out there you may adhere to (for more information about the various theories, see Millard J. Erickson's *Christian Theology*, 3rd *ed.*, pgs. 337–357)[2], the question still remains about the first cause. We live in a cause-and-effect world. If a particle heated up or moved, beginning the process of the Big Bang Theory, what caused it to heat or move in the first place? Can a ball begin to roll on its own without the existence of trees or clouds blowing wind or a human child to kick it? If there was a first living species or human being, who caused it to exist? It takes more faith to believe explanations other than a Divine Creator. Creation most obviously testifies to a Divine Creator who is outside of time and space, a Creator who spoke things into being out of nothing. Since we believe in a God who can create something out of nothing, think about what areas of your life feel formless and void? In what area is there absence of light? We can go to Him and ask Him to speak. When everything feels hopeless, remember who your God is. He's the one that makes the impossible possible (Luke 1:37).

Nothing is ever hopeless. God is grand, majestic, and powerful. He ushers forth His Word, and the impossible suddenly becomes possible. In His divine wisdom He may not answer exactly like you ask, but invite Him to work, because He is able but often waits on an invitation of the heart. If He doesn't seem to answer like you asked, keep persisting in prayer about it until you sense a firm no. If you sense a firm no, surrender and trust it. Remember this: it's easy for us to know what we would do if we had God's power, but it is impossible to know what we would do if we had God's wisdom and knowledge. This idea reminds me that there's a bigger, more eternally important story going on that I can't totally see. When my smaller story interferes with the bigger story, the answer to my prayer will be no, but it is for our very best good that it remains a no. Before He ever spoke any one thing into existence, He had the larger plan already mapped out from beginning to end.

Throughout this book you will see evidence of that concept come clearly to the surface. You will find His prophetic plan peeking out from inside some of the very first stories as if it were a treasure waiting to be uncovered by those of the appropriate generation. There are most certainly end-times treasures in Genesis—the earliest book of the Bible, the book that was written well over a thousand years before Christ ever walked the earth. And yet in Genesis there are hidden prophetic references not only to Christ but also references to some of the very end-times plans, which are confirmed by other books of the Bible, including Revelation. The prophetic pictures we will see unfold through some of the Genesis stories will enhance our understanding of current and end-times events, as well as give us a deeper understanding of the heart of Christ. I have a feeling you'll walk away from this book energized by the Spirit and more in love with Christ.

Should I Trust God's Expertise over Mine?

Why trust Him? I've heard people say, "No one cares more about your life than you do." While that may be true from a human-nature standpoint, it's not true in the big picture. Hopefully, the Holy Spirit will use this book to reveal to you the truth of the fact that He cares about you more than you care about you. That's why you can trust Him.

Do you want to know one small hint that sheds light onto the fact that He might have had everything planned out before He created anything? There are a lot of reasons I'm convinced of this. We will get into more of these reasons as we journey through this book. But since we are touching on the creation story in this chapter, I want to mention one reason that pertains to creation: you can't study created things with an open and objective mind and walk away without at least wondering if it's possible that we have an intelligent Creator. I encourage you to study created things.

Let me just mention a few for argument's sake. E. W. Bullinger wrote *Number in Scripture: Its Supernatural Design and Spiritual Significance*, which has since become a classic on many scholars' bookshelves. In a small section of this book, he discusses the design of sound. Most of us are familiar with the idea of sound waves. Sound waves are basically vibrations in the air. Visualize a line as a wave pattern (think of a line of sideways S's connected to one another). Each wave is a vibration. What Bullinger found was that each individual musical note was consistently the same unique number of wave vibrations every time it was measured.

For example, a G note might have a pattern of five waves; and an A note might have a pattern of six waves. You could measure the waves' vibrations and know which note was being heard. But that's not all. He decided to see whether sound waves correlated with light waves. Guess what happened? They did. Light waves (vibrations of light) in the air show different colors. So just like the musical note of G might have a pattern of five waves, the corresponding color with five light waves might be green. Bullinger says, "Hence there are seven colors answering to the seven musical sounds, and it is found that sounds which harmonize, correspond with colors that harmonize. While discords in color correspond with discords in music."[3] In other words, when you play a G chord on the piano, the notes that make the full chord are G, B, and D. They harmonize and give a full G sound.

Similarly, the three colors that correspond to the three notes would mix well into a beautiful color. Have you ever seen a color spectrum? It shows what happens when you mix certain colors. For instance, blue and yellow make green, which means the sound waves that correspond to the light waves that make up blue and yellow would likewise harmonize. What a great and masterful Designer we have! He did not create out of randomness. He created out of a complex, orderly, and well-thought out plan.

Bullinger also points out that gestation periods are commonly multiples of seven, according to days or weeks. For example, the mouse's gestation period is 21 days (three times seven). The cat's gestation period is 56 days (eight times seven). The dog's gestation period is 63 days (nine times seven). A human's gestation period is 280 days (forty times seven).[4] Coincidence? I think not. It is a perfectly ordered design.

When we study creation as well as Scripture, we find God to be the great mathematician who is organized and orderly in the way He moves and creates and acts. He doesn't haphazardly bring things to be. Before He brought man into existence, He had thoroughly thought through the design, seeing the future to completion before He ever said, "Let there be . . ." Redemption was prepared to be offered before sin ever happened. That's why we can trust His expertise over our own. His mind is greater. His heart is bigger. His love is truer. He doesn't enact something new without first seeing the end. The road may be hard, but it is best. He has sound waves interwoven with light waves. He has gestation periods balanced with pulse rates. He has the earth spinning at the exact angle needed to sustain life. The culmination of the plan needs all the parts to work together. We can trust Him. He does grand, majestic, beautiful work. Sometimes the process has to be heated in order to bring forth the beauty of the metal, but rest assured the beauty will come in time.

We will see things come to light in Genesis that the original human author couldn't have possibly known. We will find that the divine Spirit inspired the writers to perfectly record certain things and leave out other things so that once Jesus came as the key to unlock new mysteries of the kingdom and fulfill Old Testament Scripture, a deeper story would unfold. We will see Him all over the pages of Genesis.

CHAPTER 2

Undo Button
(Adam & Eve)

HAVE YOU EVER WANTED to undo something in your life? The regret, the could haves, should haves, and the if only I would haves. How many times have I said, "If I could just go back and do it again, I would do it differently." There are times when I want that little Microsoft Word undo button. Do you remember the choose-your-own-ending books? If you had read to a certain point and didn't like how it was turning out, you could go back and choose another ending. I loved that. There have been times where I've wanted that ability in my own life. I'm pretty sure Adam and Eve felt the same after the tree incident. Everything was perfect, but the Enemy whispered doubt about God's goodness. They bit—hook, line, and sinker. Then they fell from the perfect state they were in to a fallen one. The effects of sin contaminated like an epidemic, bringing a curse to everything it touched.

You might ask, *But why did God allow the Enemy in the garden? And why did He even set up a forbidden tree to tempt in the first place?* Good questions. I've asked questions like those a thousand times. By asking

God and pondering those questions, I've come to realize that loyalty with no opportunity to be tempted is simply mandated loyalty. The opportunity to be tempted reveals how genuine and authentic love and loyalty really are. The opportunity to veer is there to bring forth the truth of the reality inside. What is your life revealing about your loyalties and loves? Is God at the top of the list, or somewhere below yourself, your kids, or your spouse? Every day that I don't wake up and consciously commit to die to myself and live for kingdom things, I let God slip down the list, and sometimes I let Him slip really far down the list. Those are the days where I want to press the undo button. I see my loyalty and love for Him get tested every day, and too often I am found lacking.

But do you know what happens when God's loyalty and love for us are tested? The truth of His ever-pursuing love comes forth. All throughout the Bible we find Him implementing a way to allow us to come back to Him. He's the relentless Lover who never wavers in His commitment. Look at verses like these: "For the Son of Man has come to seek and to save that which was lost" (Luke 19:10 NASB); "You did not choose me, but I chose you" (John 15:16). And even in the garden we see God pursuing Adam and Eve who were actually trying to get away from God when they hid in shame after sinning. You can almost hear the pain in God's voice as He knowingly said, "Where are you?" (Genesis 3:9). He is ever the one who is relentless in loving our hearts, even when we are at our worst. Sin separates us from God and muddies our eyes and stuffs our ears, yet we find He has planned a bridge all along if we will just respond when we feel Him drawing us near.

In some ways, I have felt a glimpse of how He feels at times when He offers a bridge but we don't accept. I think about how I felt one time when a friend and I had gotten into a disagreement. There was distance between us, and I came to understand that distance wasn't worth it over something so petty. I sincerely apologized and asked for her forgiveness and expressed the fact that I didn't care about any of it anymore; I just wanted to be close again. This next point is where I began to understand how God might feel at times. My friend looked at me and said she'd accept my apology, but she'd rather not be close to me anymore. I was crushed. I had wiped the slate clean (her part and mine) and was offering a bridge back to closeness. Although God never has to apologize for anything because He never treats anyone wrongly or sins, I have the ability to feel what He feels when He makes a way to be close to Him again but we choose not to take it.

Jesus said, "No one can come to me unless the Father who sent me draws them" (John 6:44). He loves us first, draws us first, offers the bridge first. We have no merit in finding Him first. He is the relentless pursuer. We just choose what we do with His offers. Sin distances His voice and makes us put up man-made hiding places, like busyness or our pursuit of success or philanthropy to "cover" our shame. These are often the types of fig leaves we weave together to try to make ourselves feel better. How do you try to cover the shame you might feel in the sight of God? Do you try to work extra hard to impress Him? Do you try to somehow earn your worthiness? Well, I have a truth for you. All He really wants is for you to answer His question, "Where are you?" He already knows. But His question invites confession so He can let you close again. There's nothing that brings more rest and peace to the heart than true reconciliation.

This is a poem I wrote as I applied the Genesis story of the fall to my own life:

> That ole devil preys on the shame he finds
> And shackles the ones with the hiding minds.
> He confirms with wounds so deep
> That even haunt you in your sleep,
> Saying, "You'll never be quite up to par.
> There's something wrong with who you are."
> Never suspecting these words as lies, and

Replaying them over and over in time,
We place our hands into his cuffs
And let him have his way with us.
But this heart, it beats for something more,
Saying, "This is not what I was created for!"
I've been bound by shame, but I've had enough
No longer slave—I'm bought by Love.
Jesus, let me tell my heart to You
And heal the hurt he's dragged me through
Break again bones mended wrong
And from the pain, bring forth a song.
I trust the pain that You might bring;
It's a sanctifying suffering.

Isaiah 61:1 offers prophetic words about Christ. Consider these words in light of the poem: "He has sent Me to bind up the brokenhearted, to proclaim freedom for the captives and release from darkness for the prisoners."

The Problem of Sin

Genesis 3 talks in detail about this very first sin of humanity. Most of us probably know the story of Adam and Eve's temptation by the serpent pretty well, but there's one tiny detail that often gets overlooked. I want to talk about that one tiny detail today. Let's read in Genesis 3:20–21, "The man called his wife's name Eve, because she was the mother of all living. And the Lord God made for Adam and for his wife garments of skins and clothed them." Prior to this verse, they had sinned in the garden when they ate from the forbidden tree. After sinning, the man and woman realized their nakedness, hid themselves, and sewed fig leaves together as a temporary covering. God knew the leaves would not last or even truly cover them, so in verse 21, He made for them garments of skins and clothed them. Do you know where someone gets skins?

They kill animals to get skins. An animal had to be killed in order for God to make garments of skins for them. It's the very first sacrifice for sin we see in the Bible, and even at this very first sacrifice for sin, we see the death of something innocent to cover the guilty.

All throughout the Bible we see God requiring a blood sacrifice for sin, whether it was the animal sacrifice in the Old Testament or Jesus's sacrifice in the New Testament. People might say, *Why couldn't God just forgive us without demanding blood? Is blood even necessary? Couldn't He just decide to forgive us?* I've asked these questions myself. That's why I want to talk about it.

Our Creator is a good, perfect, and holy God. Sin and God can't dwell together. As image bearers of God, we are also the same in a way. Sin and humanity aren't made to go together either. When the effects of sin touch us, we feel it. We feel it each time wrong is done to us. We feel it when we are rejected and hurt by those we love. We feel it when we lose sleep and peace because of some sin we've allowed into our lives. Since the effects of sin introduced sickness and death into this world, those things affect everyone now, no matter how innocent we are. We feel the wrongness when cancer takes someone in our family. We feel it when the good die young and the evil ones go unpunished. Something wars inside our soul and screams, "This is not how it was supposed to be!" And that voice inside us is correct. This is *not* how it was supposed to be. Sin and evil lead to death and sever relationships and bring darkness and unrest.

When sin and evil entered the picture, things were no longer like they were supposed to be. God had a choice in the garden that day. He is perfectly holy, so He knew He had to rid the world of evil to fix the problem. But the problem is, we all now have evil inside of us since we are physical descendants of Adam and Eve, who invited the evil inside of them. They passed down a sin nature that is now present in all of us. And we have all caved to our sin nature at some point and committed sin. If even one ounce of sin is in us, it eventually contaminates the whole being. It ends up growing like a dangerous fungus if left untreated. We fall short of the standard from the very start and can't get rid of the fungus on our own. That's where the problem lies. So, yes, He could rid the world of evil with the snap of His fingers, but He would also have to rid the world of you and me in the process. Evil already has its hold on us in our inherited sin nature from Adam.

Think about the most evil person you know of that ever lived. That's the potential effect of sin on a life. Sin can make a person pretty terrible in a hurry, can't it? Today, the lifespan of a person is only a little over one hundred years at the most. Some people let sin reign wildly in their lives and other people try to keep it at bay the best they can. But everyone has sin in them. Unless God offered a real remedy for sin, it would be in all humans for eternity.

Think about what sin can grow to do within a normal lifespan. Now, think about what even the tiniest remnant of sin might grow to do over the span of eternity. Even the smallest sin left untreated would eventually, over the course of eternity, make us all monsters. Pretty soon, heaven would no longer be heaven. It would be evil like much of what our world has turned into today.

We needed a real remedy, not just lip service. Christ died to pay the price for our sins and resurrected proving His power to defeat sin and death. This is important because His resurrection proves He has the power to defeat the Enemy and every sin and evil. His resurrection is a deposit guaranteeing He has the power to make everything right again in the end, and He will do it. When we accept His free gift of grace to us for salvation, He puts the Holy Spirit inside of us to help sanctify us for the rest of this earthly life until He will one day raise us up "imperishable" (1 Cor. 15:42, 52). Because there was a real remedy offered, heaven can truly be without sin, evil, pain, and heartache for eternity.

I say all that to say the Enemy and sin have left their mark on us, and we are doomed without a Savior. But Scripture shows us God had a plan for our redemption through His Son, Jesus, from the very start.

As Americans we like instant, quick, and easy, don't we? Because of this tendency of ours, it's natural to ask why He didn't go ahead and send His Son closer to the beginning if He had it all mapped out rather than waiting thousands of years and implementing animal sacrifices first. I believe it is because God knows the value of time. Wisdom comes over time. Understanding comes over time. Maturity and intelligence come over time. Most of the really valuable things demand the ingredient of time. In hindsight we can see what God was doing. He was divinely writing the Old Testament by painting physical pictures and visuals and stories that would all point forward to be shadows of heavenly things and shadows of His Son who would one day come.

Because we have the Old Testament, Jesus can be more glorified in our hearts, and we can now see how Jesus was the greater Adam and the greater Moses. Jesus was the greater Joseph and the greater David. All of the stories of the Old Testament point forward to have their fulfillment in Jesus. And all of the stories of the Old Testament tell us something about God's plan. I wonder if God knew how much evil would increase toward these end times and how hardened people would become to the truth, so He took the time to paint an absolutely genius picture of the Savior and His plan through the many stories. He was patient through the slow, long process knowing He wanted none to perish and all to come to repentance.

Maybe He knew the intellect of mankind in these last days would need to be convinced that God was more of a genius than any of us. Maybe He knew there would be some of us who would be drawn by the fact that He wove a story so perfectly and with such imagery over thousands of years and through many writers on various continents to make one big inspired book telling the same story, called the Bible. It is a book that continually points the way to salvation through His Son (often without the Old Testament human author knowing it) and records prophecies given by God that all came true in Jesus's first coming or point forward to events surrounding Jesus's second coming.

God is long-suffering in His way of bringing to salvation all who will come. He took the time to paint the pictures and stories of the Old Testament over time. The Old Testament contains the physical representations of the spiritual realities found in the New Testament. Let me say it another way. The Old Testament records the physical stories that actually happened so they could be picture lessons to help us understand the spiritual realities under the new covenant in Jesus.

Before Jesus could come as the ultimate sacrifice, a physical picture had to be painted of a lesser animal sacrifice that humans would try on their own. It was necessary for God's people to feel the weight of the law and the weight of the requirements on their own shoulders so they could one day fully appreciate what the Son of God would do for them.

Hebrews 9:22 says, "Indeed, under the law almost everything is purified with blood, and without the shedding of blood there is no forgiveness of sins." But what's significant about a sacrifice that had blood?

Leviticus 17:11 says, "For the life of the flesh is in the blood, and I have given it for you on the altar to make atonement for your souls, for it is the blood that makes atonement by the life." The life is in the blood. In essence God will accept the innocent life of one for another, but something must die for the sin committed. That's why you see so many animal sacrifices in the Old Testament. God planned long ago that He would send His Son as the eternal sacrifice once and for all. In the meantime, the people of God had to repeatedly sacrifice innocent, unblemished animals to atone for their sin. All of those sacrifices pointed to and had faith in the power of the Greater Sacrifice to come—Jesus. I wonder if God put into place a human-animal closeness so His people would begin to experience the weight of what sin requires.

In Genesis 3:20–21, the name given to the woman is interesting. It says, "The man called his wife's name Eve, because she was the mother of all living. And the Lord God made for Adam and for his wife garments of skins and clothed them." The name given to her is interesting because up to this point in Scripture, Adam and Eve had no children of their own, yet he calls her "the mother of all living." Obviously Eve had displayed some motherly tendencies with the animals living in the garden or he wouldn't have named her something so personal. We women tend to treat our animals like our babies, don't we? And then *the very next verse* is when Scripture says God made them garments of skins to clothe their nakedness. Where do garments of skins come from? Animals. One of Eve's animal babies had to die because of Adam's and her sin.

Now, for an animal lover like me, that's giving *weight* to sin. My heart feels ripped out when I think about an animal having to die for my sin. When I let myself think about a sacrifice (ultimately Jesus) having to die for my sin, I start to grasp the weight of it. I think Adam and Eve were able to grasp the weight of it too. Sin is not free or without consequences. I suspect that as a society we have subtly come to believe that sin isn't that big of a deal just because the patience of God is long-suffering. But it *is* a big deal. It always steals. It always takes something away or destroys something good. Sin has weight whether you see it immediately or not. Thankfully we get to accept Jesus, the Lamb of God, to take away our sins once and for all. How I love God for loving us enough to be willing to send His Son to die as our sacrifice in order save us. Because of Jesus, when He comes to rid the world of evil, we who honor Him as King of our lives will be spared because His blood has paid our price.

What's more is that our Ultimate Sacrifice didn't just die, He rose from the dead. So, by overcoming death, Jesus is the sacrifice that *also* proved His ability to break sin's super powers of death and evil. Since

Jesus has always existed (see John 1), then came to earth in human form, died, rose from the dead, and now lives forever, His sacrifice lives forever to make atonement for those who choose to follow Him. It reaches back into history saving those who had faith in the sacrifices that pointed forward. It reaches the present and it reaches the future. Jesus is the perfect sacrifice for all who will believe. And since He proved His ability to conquer death and evil, He can enable us to break free from the sin in our lives that entangles us if we lean into Him for help. He can free us from the power and addictive bondage of sin and give us victory after victory over it, sanctifying us little by little until He comes again to rid the entire world of evil forever. We won't be perfectly sinless this side of heaven, but that's why He sent His Spirit to dwell within us to help us and guide us in the sanctification process. So let's be careful not to quench Him. He is for us, not against us (Rom. 8:31).

Christ, the Second Adam

First Corinthians 15 describes Christ as the second Adam. In addition to making his point about Adam, Paul is also giving us an example of how to study Old Testament Scripture by looking for typologies. By typologies, I mean Christ and God's plan are often prefigured or symbolized by stories, people, or concepts in the Old Testament. Paul reveals that Christ is the second Adam, and a better Adam to redeem the role of the first one. The first Adam ate of the tree and brought the curse and death. The second Adam (Christ) took on the curse so those who would "eat" of Him as the Bread of Life would indeed find life. What the first Adam set into motion, Christ, the second Adam, brought power and promise to undo.

The curse of the first Adam that chains us to the Evil One and to sin by our fallen nature has to be broken if we want eternal life with God. It's popular in our current culture for people to say that many roads lead to heaven. The world wants us to deny that there is only *one* way to heaven. But if Jesus was who He said He was, then we have to accept His words as truth, and if His words are truth, then all ways *don't* lead to eternal life. Jesus said, "I am *the* way, *the* truth, and *the* life. No one comes to the Father except through Me" (John 14:6, italics mine). Why is no other way good enough? Of course, it has to do with the eternality of His blood being able to cover past, present, and future sin. But there's something more.

Christ came to earth as fully God and fully man. He came as the better Adam, rectifying the curse rather than bringing a curse. He spoke with wisdom and authority on earth and did many miracles demonstrating that He was the Son of God and the promised Messiah who had the power to reverse the effects of the fall. Each miracle was a way of saying, "Do you see? I have the ultimate power to reverse the curses you now know and live with. Believe in Me. Follow Me. Trust Me. I will one day restore everything that's been lost to those who will give their lives to follow Me." The sick were brought to Him, and He healed them. The dead were presented to Him, and He raised them back to life. The hungry came, and He fed them. The demon-possessed crossed His path, and He cast the evil spirits out of them giving them peace and sanity again. He didn't right *every* wrong or heal *every* person in all the cities He walked through. It wasn't a blanket cure. But when He encountered the ones who would believe, He did those things to confirm to their softened hearts that He was the One they had been waiting for. He was the One with the power to overcome the curse that came after the very first sin in Genesis.

Bible scholar Arthur Pink has made seven correlations between the first Adam and the second Adam that are worth noting. God's attention to detail within His plan is profound. The first Adam brought seven curses as a result of the fall in Genesis 3. The second Adam (Christ) brought seven reversals to those curses. Both are outlined in the chart below:

The Seven Curses upon Adam	**The Seven Reversals in Christ**
1. The ground was cursed.	1. Christ was "made a *curse* for us" (Gal. 3:3).
2. In sorrow, man was to eat of it all the days of his life.	2. So thoroughly was He acquainted with grief, He was designated "the man of *sorrows*" (Isa. 53:3).
3. Thorns and thistles it was to bring forth.	3. In order that we might know how literally the Holy One bore in His body the consequences of man's sin, we read, "Then came Jesus forth wearing the crown of *thorns*" (John 19:5).
4. In the sweat of his face man was to eat his bread.	4. Corresponding with the sweat of His face in which the first Adam was to eat his bread, we learn concerning the second Adam, "And His *sweat* was as it were great drops of blood falling down to the ground" (Luke 22:44).
5. Unto dust man was to return.	5. Just as the first Adam was to return to the dust, so the cry of the last Adam, in that wonderful prophetic Psalm, was, "Thou hast brought Me into the *dust* of the death" (Ps. 22:15).

6. A flaming sword barred his way to the tree of life.	6. The *sword* of justice which barred the way to the tree of life was sheathed in the side of God's Son on the cross, for of old, Jehovah had said, "Awake, O *sword*, against My shepherd, and against the man that is My Fellow" (Zech. 13:7).
7. There was the execution of God's threat that in the day man partook of the forbidden fruit he should surely die.	7. The counterpart of God's original threat to Adam, namely, spiritual death (for he did not die physically the same day), which is the separation of the soul from God, is witnessed in that most solemn of all cries, "My God, My God, Why hast Thou forsaken Me?" (Matt. 27:46).[5]

I'll add one more: Adam disobeyed by eating fruit off the tree; Christ obeyed by sacrificing Himself on a tree in our place. Christ, only Christ, fully bore the curse in every way. When the fullness of time is complete, He will come in power and glory and reverse it all completely and forever.

Prophecy in Genesis 3

In Genesis 3:15, God says to the serpent, "I will put enmity between you and the woman, and between your offspring and her offspring; he shall bruise your head, and you shall bruise his heel." If we pay attention to detail, we realize how odd it is that the offspring or seed is considered the woman's rather than the man's. In Scripture, the lineage is traced through the man, and our names are changed to the man's name in a marriage or adoption. And yet God prophetically says to the *woman* that there will be enmity between her offspring and the serpent's offspring. God was already hinting toward the virgin birth of Christ. Mary, a virgin, gave birth to Christ, the offspring of the woman spoken about in Genesis 3. The woman's offspring is Christ; the serpent's offspring is the Antichrist.

Already, in Genesis 3, we learn there will be an age-long battle between good and evil—Christ and the Antichrist, but also between God's people and the people of the world under the influence of the Enemy. God's original people, the Jewish people of Israel, have been taunted immensely throughout the ages. The Holocaust. Persecution. Eviction from the land God gave them. Look at history and you will find Israel and God's people have been a target through the generations because there's a war going on that does not begin against flesh and blood, but it is a war initiated in the heavenlies that bleeds through to the physical. The Enemy is against Christ and His people.

There's a constant struggle throughout the timeline of history and a constant struggle that surrounds each child of God. Do you feel it at times? Do you see it bleed out into your reality? Do you hear the whispers of lies that try to make you feel insecure and fearful in order to keep you from walking out His calling on your life with courage and boldness? We give part of ourselves to the devil when we give him our ear and believe him. Our beliefs always end up controlling our actions. Let's stop fighting against ourselves and God's angels who are fighting for us in the spiritual realm, and kill the lies so we can overpower the real Enemy of our lives instead of ourselves.

The serpent didn't first come to Adam, but came to Eve because she was the carrier of the seed. The serpent went straight for the one who could most thwart God's plan. If you're following Christ, the devil will want to thwart God's plan to be done through you too. Stand firm. Walk in faith, not in fear. Tell the insecurities to sit down and hush. Step out of the boat and let your life matter for the right side of the war. You are gifted and you are called. Yes, you. So walk it out.

The last part of the verse in Genesis 3 is speaking to the serpent: "He shall bruise your head, and you shall bruise his heel." Scholars say the image of the serpent striking the heel was fulfilled at the moment of the cross. It had appeared the Enemy had won, when he crucified the Son of God who was supposed to save His people from their sin. As Jesus hung there on the cross, the serpent probably gloated thinking he won. But the story wasn't over. Jesus arose from the grave, defeating His own death and showing power over the Enemy and the curse. But prophesies rarely have just one fulfillment. We often see them have multiple fulfillments.

One day we will see Christ bruise the head of the serpent once again to a greater degree. We will get into this in more detail in later chapters, but after the great tribulation of the end times, Revelation says Christ will bind the Enemy up for a thousand years (this period is called the millennium). That will be the second fulfillment for the bruise to the serpent's head. Revelation 20 says that after the serpent has been bound for a thousand years (the millennium), he must be released for a "little while" in order to deceive the nations one more time. I believe this time of deceiving will be the final test, revealing who are true seekers of Christ and who are only halfhearted seekers. But after the "little while" is over, Christ will cast the Enemy into the lake of fire to be tormented forever. The curse will be broken completely forever for everyone throughout time who has persevered in Christ. His head will finally be crushed for good. Satan will be defeated. Look at the references to "the ancient serpent" in the verses in Revelation 20:

> Then I saw an angel coming down from heaven, holding in his hand the key to the bottomless pit and a great chain. And he seized the dragon, that ancient serpent, who is the devil and Satan, and bound him for a thousand years, and threw him into the pit, and shut it

and sealed it over him, so that he might not deceive the nations any longer, until the thousand years were ended. After that he must be released for a little while. . . . And when the thousand years are ended, Satan will be released from his prison and will come out to deceive the nations that are at the four corners of the earth, God and Magog, to gather them for battle; their number is like the sand of the sea. And they marched up over the broad plain of the earth and surrounded the camp of the saints and the beloved city, but fire came down from heaven and consumed them, and the devil who had deceived them was thrown into the lake of fire and sulfur where the beast and the false prophet were, and they will be tormented day and night forever and ever. (Rev. 20:1–3, 7–10)

Have you allowed your life to be on the side of good or evil? Of Christ or of the Enemy? We know which one will win in the end, so choose the right team and jump all the way in. The battle is fierce, but let's be the valiant warriors who are loyal and brave, conquering fears and insecurities for the sake of our part in the battle. A life lived in surrender to Christ's leadership is worth more than you may ever know this side of heaven. Ask Him to be your General today if you haven't already. Salvation and life is in Christ alone.

CHAPTER 3

Worthiness
(Cain & Abel)

ARE YOU A HIGH achiever? Do you get a rush when you check things off your to-do list? When you mow the lawn or clean the house, are you a little offended when the person you live with doesn't notice? I am all of those things too.

I used to work in the corporate world before I quit to pursue ministry full-time. That career ladder for me was a rush! I struggle with what Brené Brown calls hustling for my worthiness[6] or trying to earn my worthiness. Every promotion made me feel like I was on cloud nine. But every criticism made me crash and burn. It was a roller coaster. My significance was tied up in my performance. I was a type of Pharisee who was letting my actions control my significance rather than letting the grace of Christ control my significance.

That's what a gospel of morality, where you try to earn your significance, will do to you. It sucks you into a cycle of the pressure of being "good enough" and "achieving enough" every day. It's hard for me to remember I can't *earn* His love. I *want* to earn it, because if I can earn it, then God owes me something and I'm given a little control. When a person is an employee at a company, they show up and do the work, and legally, the employer then owes that person payment for their labor. We are used to this idea, but how often do we try to use it on God? When we take an honest look at Christianity in America, the answer is that we try to use this idea on God more often than not. That's why people get so offended at God when crisis comes in their life. People often assume that if they have been a good person or given God their lives, God owes them wealth, prosperity, and a good life on earth. Since all of the twelve disciples were martyred or exiled for their faith and Job was tested severely, I'm going to say that's not the way it works.

Do you know how the New Testament describes the gospel? It describes it as "the gospel of *grace*" (Acts 20:24, italics mine). First Timothy 2:1 exhorts us by saying, "You then, my child, be strong in the *grace* that is in Christ Jesus" (NRSV, italics mine). Notice, it does not say be strong in morality, though being a good person is good. It says be strong in the *grace* that is in Christ Jesus. He knows that grace changes us from the inside out, not from the outside in like we think morality will. Morality may make us appear like we are good, but it has no power to change the heart, which is the core of who we are. Understanding, believing, and trusting the grace of Christ brings a new heart. The writer of Hebrews has a firm statement for us. Out of all of the instruction that could have been chosen, the most important reminder was, "See to it that no one misses the grace of God" (Heb. 12:15 NIV). Grace is foundational to Christianity.

What is grace? I've often heard it defined as "undeserved favor." That's a good definition, but it still took me a long time to truly grasp grace. Before I grasped grace, there were times when I would be proud of myself for accepting Christ as if I had somehow initiated it. But as I started grasping grace, I began to see verses in the Bible where Jesus said, "You did not choose Me, but I chose you" (John 15:16), and verses where Paul explains, "For *by grace* you have been saved through faith. *And this is not your own doing*; it is the gift of God, *not a result of works*, so that no one may boast" (Eph. 2:8, italics mine), and "So too at the present time there is a remnant, chosen by grace. But if it is by grace, it is no longer on the basis of works; otherwise grace would no longer be grace" (Rom. 11:5–6).

Much of Christianity in America sets grace aside as a side note of the religion to use at times but not as the main part. Christianity in America is, instead, infiltrated with a version of Christianity that turns it into a gospel of morality. And a gospel of morality is powerless.

To make Christianity a gospel of morality makes it like every other religion. Every other religion has a gospel of morality. What originally set Christianity apart is that it *wasn't* a gospel of morality. But somehow in our culture, all of the religions have fallen into one big melting pot and have gotten mushed together, causing this form of Christianity to emerge here in places.

Other religions teach concepts like doing five steps, and then one can gain enlightenment or living rightly enough according to the Four Noble Truths for a person to obtain Nirvana. In every other religion the pressure is all on you. You are your own savior or failure. Somehow Christianity has morphed into this, but it was never supposed to be this way. What we will find today in our study is that Cain tried to live by a gospel contrary to God's, and it didn't work out well for him.

Most of us are probably at least familiar with the story of Cain and Abel. If you aren't, stop and take a second to read Genesis 4:1–16. Abel was a keeper of sheep, and Cain was a worker of the ground. Cain brought an offering of fruit from the ground to the Lord, and Abel brought to the Lord the firstborn of his flock and of their fat portions. Scripture says that the Lord had regard for Abel and his animal offering but no regard for Cain and his fruit offering. But why? Before digging in deeper, doesn't something in you sympathize with Cain like, "Poor guy. He was trying his best"? But his best wasn't good enough if it was not what the Lord had asked. Neither is ours.

Scholars say it is safe to infer from various details in Scripture that God had made it clear to both of them what kind of offering He required. Both guys knew the Lord required the blood of an animal, but only one gave it. Remember Hebrews 9:22? "Without the shedding of blood, there is no forgiveness." And yet Cain insisted on bringing God the "fruit" from his own labors as an offering instead. Abel's animals pretty much raised themselves. The lambs had mothers that took care of all of their needs. Abel just watched them to keep predators away if they came. But Cain, on the other hand, probably worked his back to soreness from cultivating fields, growing crops and fruit, and then harvesting it. In Cain's mind, he probably thought, *I'm doing way more work for the Lord's offering than my brother, so there's no way I won't be more acceptable to God than him! God is going to be so proud.* In other words, he insisted on coming to God on the basis of personal worthiness rather than having faith in what God had said.

We are sometimes the same, aren't we? How many times have you heard someone say, "I'm a good person, so I think I'm going to heaven"? We insist on doing things in order to earn our own worthiness before Him instead of trusting in the blood for our worthiness. Here's the problem, though, according to Timothy Keller: A moral-based gospel for salvation can only produce two things in us, and neither are good on their own. A moral-based gospel for salvation will either produce (1) pride and arrogance or (2) overwhelming despair. Let's use the Ten Commandments as our standard. (1) Either we look at the Ten Commandments as our standard for salvation and get puffed up with pride at how well we have kept them, or (2) we look at the Ten Commandments as our standard for salvation and realize how far we have fallen short, and we become overwhelmed with hopeless despair. The end result of a gospel of morality for salvation or significance is either pride and arrogance or hopeless despair. Neither are good on their own.[7] The first response is what Christ detested about the Pharisees. In fact, when we read through the four Gospel accounts, we find that Christ saved his harshest words, not for the sinner, but for the puffed up, morally religious groups like the Pharisees. The second response of hopeless despair only becomes good if it drives us to realize our desperate need for a Savior.

Timothy Keller explained, "Only Christianity destroys both pride *and* despair. Christianity first shows you a law that has to be totally fulfilled, destroying your pride. Then Christianity shows you a Savior who has totally fulfilled it, getting rid of your despair."[8]

When we are trying to earn our own worthiness, our worthiness is hinged upon how well things go or how much people or God appreciate us. That's why people who do this feel so much pressure for things to go right and get very upset if those things don't go just right. When the Lord refused to accept Cain's offering, Scripture says he became so angry that he murdered his brother Abel.

No doubt the fruit Cain offered was probably some of the most beautiful that he could cultivate from the ground. And there's no question that giving to God this amount of fruit was costly to him in hard labor, because the ground was cursed back in Genesis 3. The curse on the ground meant that man would now have to "labor and toil" in order to bring fruit from the ground. It wasn't necessarily that honoring God with his labor was bad, but that his faith was in his own efforts rather than in the blood that God provided life to through the animal. It's almost as if Cain couldn't make sense of atonement in his head. I can just hear him reasoning, "How can blood of an animal with a life breathed into it by *God*, and not grown by us, even be an acceptable offering *from* us? The mother of a sheep is more responsible for sustaining the sheep's life than my brother Abel is! How is *that* an offering? How can *that* make *me* worthy to God? My beautiful fruit *I* have cultivated is going to be so much better." And so Cain insisted on giving to God out of his own personal worthiness.

The Scripture says that when the Lord had no regard for Cain's offering, he was "very angry and his face fell" (v. 5). Anger is often what we exhibit when our best isn't accepted or appreciated the way we think it should be. Anger is normally a secondary emotion. The primary emotion is usually more vulnerable (such as hurt) and therefore, in order to act or feel tough, we often jump over the more vulnerable emotion and go straight to a less vulnerable one such as anger. Anger usually feels more like we are in control and feels less personal to our weakness. Have you ever noticed that when someone hits a raw spot in your heart, it's so much easier to be angry about it than to explain to the person why it hurt your feelings so deeply? Anger is less emotionally risky. When anger is being used to mask a more vulnerable layer underneath, it is unhealthy and often destructive to relationships.

Obviously Cain's pride and feelings of significance were hurt when God rejected his offering, but he jumped to anger and sulked instead of talking about it when the Lord asked him why he was angry (Genesis 4:6). I wonder to myself how things might have been different if Cain would have just talked it out with the Lord that day. But Cain wasn't willing to address the layers underneath, and God had been clear about what was acceptable in regard to the offering. Like his mother, Eve (They both had fruit issues, didn't they?), Cain had decided he knew better than God and would take matters into his own hands. By the very fact that he wouldn't respond to God's question asking why he was angry, we see that Cain still thought he knew better than God and felt he had been treated unfairly.

Later in the Bible, 1 John 3:12 calls Abel's actions righteous and Cain's evil. Evil? Really? In God's view, yes. Isaiah 64:6 (NIV) says, "All of us have become like one who is unclean, and all our righteous acts are like filthy rags." In other words, all of our ways to earn our own righteousness before God are like filth to Him. But Hebrews 11:4 says, "*By faith* Abel offered to God a more acceptable sacrifice than Cain, through which he was commended as righteous, God commending him by accepting his gifts" (italics mine). Faith isn't believing *in* God. Even Satan believes *in* God. Faith is *believing God.* When we choose *faith* in what God says, believing Him over everything else, it pleases God. Hebrews 11:6 says, "*Without faith* it is impossible to please God" (italics mine). In the case of Cain and Abel, it was only by *faith* in what God had said about the ability of a blood sacrifice to atone that they could be made clean. It's the same way today. We put our faith in the eternal blood of Jesus, our sacrificial Lamb of God, to make us righteous before God. It takes faith to trust that what God says is accurate over what we think might be logically accurate. Because His ways are not our ways, we logically reason that we should obtain righteousness by earning it. God says we obtain righteousness through the blood of Jesus when we accept it by faith. May we only ever boast in the Lord (1 Corinthians 1:26–31).

My own "earning it" mentality has surfaced during many Christian counseling sessions. Thankfully God led me to a Christian counselor who deeply understands the concept of faith in the blood and not works in order to obtain righteousness. When I first started seeing her, I told her I felt tired and worn out and couldn't see much I had actually accomplished that was worthy of noting. It felt like I was spinning my wheels, giving everything 100 percent but not doing anything for God or people that seemed good enough. It was a time in my life when I had experienced some hard things and needed help dealing with those, but in the midst of them, there was this constant feeling of pressure and fear of not being good enough that always seemed to be present, vibrating through every situation like the bass undertones to a song. These constant feelings had been present many years. It was nothing new. It just became too much for me to bear when life wasn't going as planned.

When my counselor asked me how I was feeling that day, I replied, "Can I be honest? I'm exhausted, and yet I feel like I *should* be doing more." I continued to list the things I felt like I *should* be doing but could never quite do well enough. There were a lot of shoulds. Finally, I confessed, "I just feel like I am never enough, even though no one has ever told me that, and—" She interjected, "Good. I'm glad you're realizing that." I stopped talking mid-sentence because I was confused and looked at her. She has a habit of dropping statements like that in the room and it takes a full minute or two for my brain to catch up and understand. Once I realized what she was saying in regard to the way of the cross, I responded, "Oh. I see."

She continued with, "I think what I'm hearing from you is that you feel a lot of pressure in life—too much to bear on your own." I agreed.

As we talked through it that day, I started to realize that all the pressure I had on myself was from myself. I was striving for my own fig leaves of worthiness before God and others instead of resting in the righteous robe of worthiness that Christ had already placed around my shoulders through His sacrifice just waiting for me to fully receive it.

It takes a long time to undo the kind of earning-oriented thinking I was used to. It takes a long time to understand that the results aren't up to us. All God requires of us is persistent dependence. He is the one who grows any kingdom seeds we sow. The eternal results aren't up to us, so the pressure isn't on us. The more I've learned to rest in the worthiness Christ gives me, the freer I've become to truly walk through life in the seemingly odd giftings Christ has given me.

Now there's room to fail, and it's ok. The results don't reflect so heavily upon my significance. I stay faithful, and He works in the unseen things I can't see. The kind of pressure I knew before was debilitating and squelched my creativity. So, the more I've come along in this freedom, the more I've noticed that creativity has been unleashed in me as well. I'm realizing we were meant to be free from the pressure of earning our own worthiness, and I'm seeing that we function most fully by living in freedom from it.

Analogies help me remember things better. No analogy is perfect, but I think this one will get the point across. Imagine God's church likened to a car that requires gas, yet we are selling diesel instead. The car is saying, "Only gas will work," but we say, "No, no! Diesel is going to be better! It's refined longer and it costs more; it's *got* to be better." So we put diesel in a car that requires gas, and what happens? The diesel eventually destroys the engine of the car.

God says, "Only blood will work," but we say, "No, no. My good works for You will be better. They cost me more, so they've *got* to be better! Watch what I can do! My deeds are going to impress you so much more than blood! *This* is going to make me worthy and righteous before you and before people!"

But God knows that if He lets us earn our own worthiness with works, it will destroy the church just like diesel would destroy a gas-operated car. What happens when we set out to earn our own worthiness or righteousness in a church setting? We start comparing ourselves with everyone around us so we can ensure we are worthy. We try to one-up the person next to us so we can be loved more than them or chosen over them. We look down on people who can't do things as great as we can. Some of us only associate with those who are better than us because we think they might help make us better—and we use them as a stepping stone rather than loving them.

Some of us may be inclined to the opposite situation. Some of us only feel better about ourselves when we associate with those who are worse than we are—which isn't actually love, either, since we need those people to stay "less than" us, instead of truly wishing the best for them. And all of those things destroy the unity and love for the church. I hate to admit I've done some of these very things.

I long for a body of believers where no one is threatened by anyone else's successes or giftings. But that can only happen when each of us has our faith in the right place—in God's work, not in ourselves. Only then are we free to love.

You can see evidence of this scarcity mentality in Cain. When he tried to earn his own righteousness by offering a gift of his own labor and God rejected it, Cain burned with jealousy toward his brother Abel. Perhaps God's rejection threatened Cain's perception of self-worth and made him feel inclined to do "whatever it took" to be first. He killed his brother Abel because Abel's offering was accepted as a more excellent sacrifice than his own.

When our worth is wrapped up in our performance, we will do the same thing. We may not murder anyone, but we will do the same thing in more subtle and socially acceptable ways. We might leave that person out of our circle or talk badly about them or judge them in our hearts to justify our own shortcomings. All of these actions bring disunity to the body of Christ.

You might be saying to yourself, *But hang on. Aren't there a lot of verses in the New Testament about doing good works?* Yes. In fact, James 2:17 says that faith is considered to be dead or non-existent if it is not accompanied by works. If you really have faith in something and really believe something, your actions will follow. If you say you have faith in something or believe something, but your actions don't align with what you say you believe, you probably don't actually believe it deep down.

We can totally fool ourselves too. If you would have asked if I believed I could earn my own worthiness, I would have told you, "Of course not! Only Jesus can make me worthy and righteous." But I realized that even though I could say all the right things, I didn't really believe them. In the hidden caverns of my heart, I still believed I needed to earn His love and the love of others.

I had to have many nights confessing to the Lord in prayer that I must not actually believe what I say since I kept feeling like I hadn't earned Him "enough." I kept feeling like He was disappointed in me and probably wouldn't listen to me or do anything special for me as long as I was unsuccessful in ministry. But over time I learned to ask Him to give me a greater measure of faith to believe, and, for the first time in my life, I feel free.

I still struggle in this area from time to time, but God and I have prayer history on that subject now. So, when I begin to feel overwhelmed and feel as if all my worthiness depends on what I'm about to do, I can send up a quick prayer like this: *Father, remind me who I am to You in Christ. Remind me that I'm already worthy because of Him. You love me. It's going to be okay no matter how this turns out. And You can bear fruit for Your kingdom in this* even *if I fail because fruit comes by the work of the Spirit, not by* my *own might or power.* It's funny how a quick prayer like that can make all the tension and stress subside. Sometimes we just have to stop and remember truth.

My relationships are changing now too. I'm beginning to see people through lenses of grace and love rather than through lenses of condemnation and competition. The latter never changed anybody. But grace and love always have the power in Christ to change people for the better. I want a life of faith that brings this sort of fruit. The irony is, if you try to give God fruit in order to earn your own worthiness, it will be rejected, but if you give God faith, your life will also naturally bring forth fruit. Where you find faith, you will find actions; and where you find these actions in faith, you will find fruit at some point.

If you're having trouble believing what you know is true, just know faith is often a deliberate commitment to believe at first. In his book, *Gleanings in Genesis*, Arthur Pink discusses this kind of deliberate faith:

> This is precisely what constitutes saving faith: It is believing God's Word *and acting on it.* Consider an illustration in proof: "He said

unto Simon, Launch out into the deep, and let down your nets for a draught. And Simon answering said unto Him, "Master, we have toiled all the night, and have taken nothing: *nevertheless at Thy Word* I will let down the net" (Luke 5:4–5). Faith is more than an intellectual assent. Faith is the committal of ourselves to God's Word. Faith necessarily involves volition, "*I will let* down the net." Faith flies in the face of all carnal reasonings, feelings and experience and says, "*Nevertheless at Thy Word* I will." Abel then took God at His Word, offered his sacrifice by faith and was accepted and pronounced righteous.[9]

What God says is true, no matter how backward it may seem sometimes in this fast-paced world of earning, performing, and celebrity status. Only by resting in Him will we find true peace.

CHAPTER 4

The End Times
(Enoch, Methuselah & Noah)

DO YOU BELIEVE GOD knows all things that are going to happen in the future? The majority of those who adhere to Christianity do believe God is omniscient (all-knowing). If we don't believe God knows what will happen in the future, then we can't be absolutely sure about His promises. If God doesn't know the future, then how does He know or how is He sure He will win the war against evil in the end? He couldn't know for sure. Therefore, Christians typically believe He is omniscient, knowing past, present, and future.

In addition to fulfilled prophecy, there are many verses in Scripture that support the idea of His omniscience too. Here are a few:

- "Before I formed you in the womb I knew you, and before you were born I consecrated you; I appointed you a prophet to the nations" (Jer. 1:5).
- "Even before a word is on my tongue, behold, O Lord, you know it altogether" (Ps. 139:4).

- Jesus knew Peter would deny Him three times before the rooster crowed (Matt. 26:34).
- "Remember this and stand firm . . . I am God, and there is none like me, declaring the end from the beginning and from ancient times things not yet done" (Is. 46:8–10).

Since God knows the future, we know He can be faithful to His promises because He has already seen them come. But this causes a small problem for people when it comes to election. They say, "If God knew what was going to happen, why did He create certain people, knowing they were going to turn evil or never come to salvation? Why did He create Adam knowing he was going to sin? Why did God create a good angelic being that He knew would fall and become Satan?" We have a problem, right? Stop reading this book for a minute and flip open to Romans 9:10–24 in your Bible.

This might be one of the most challenging chapters in the whole Bible for me. That passage in Scripture says God creates some whom He knows will become vessels of wrath and some whom He knows will become vessels of mercy. Why? Why even create the ones He can foresee will become vessels of wrath? Why would He create a good being that He knew would turn and become Satan while also creating good beings that He knew would become Paul and Timothy and Mother Teresa? Yes, there's the freewill argument, but I think there's more to it. The freewill argument basically says if God created humans who would never have the ability to go wrong, they would pretty much be robots. Nothing would be a genuine choice. They would already be preprogrammed with no freedom to deter from the programming. We would love God and do good because we had to, not because we chose to. But what would be another reason why God would persist in creating beings He could foresee would go wayward?

I don't know fully. But I do know His wisdom is higher than mine, and somehow in all of it, He knew we couldn't truly know joy without first knowing sorrow. We couldn't truly know love without knowing loss.

If there was no evil in the plan, there would be no opportunity for anyone to be heroic, courageous, or brave. There would be no opportunity for us to know sacrificial love. If everything was always perfect, everything would just be half-realized. In addition, we could never know the depth of the love of God without evil present in this world. God proved His love for us by sacrificing His Son to pay the way for our guilty souls to get back to Him. That's a depth of love we could not know otherwise.

All of the real commendable qualities in a person only grow with a contrasting backdrop of evil. We will spend eternity with Christ in an incorruptible world one day with incorruptible souls (1 Cor. 15:52; 1 Peter 1:4), but something within me tells me He needed us to know the value of the goodness we will find there, and we could only fully appreciate it by experiencing evil first. So, yes, we believe God is omniscient, knowing everything (both good and evil) that is going to happen. And it's because He has known it all from beginning to end that we can find hidden treasures in His Word that He divinely inspired to be there, even though the human writer inscribing the words could not have known at the time. There are hidden treasures even within people's names in the Bible.

Names in the Bible are highly significant. The culture we live in today doesn't have the same emphasis on name meanings as our ancestors once had, but back then, a person's name was everything. And for the people of God, God often revealed to the mother or father what name He wanted for their child. God did this with Mary for Jesus (Matt. 1:20–21; Jesus means "savior"), and He did it in many other cases throughout history because He knew the names would help tell the story.

The story of each person's life recorded in the Bible is historical (meaning it actually happened), and yet while each story literally happened in history, the story can simultaneously be a prophetic picture of events to come. So, in the Bible, there are constant layers, perfectly intertwining to tell a greater story. The more I study the Bible, the more I realize God is a literary genius.

Genealogies have been recorded in the Bible throughout time so there would be historical record of the lineage of God's chosen people, Israel. Occasionally though you'll find something more within the genealogies. Chapter 3 of this book ended with Cain killing Abel. They were both sons of Adam and Eve, but since Cain was banished and Abel was killed, there had to be another son for God's people (and ultimately, Jesus, our Messiah) to come through. Genesis 5:3–4 says Adam had other sons and daughters after Cain and Abel, but Seth was the son in his own likeness, after his image. So, the rest of the chapter proceeds with the lineage of God's people from Adam to Seth to Enosh (not to be confused with Enoch, who walked with God) to Kenan to Mahalalel to Jared to Enoch to Methuselah to Lamech, and finally to Noah and his three sons. Did you fall asleep yet? Well, wake back up, because this is about to get good.

Perhaps you have heard the phrase "as old as Methuselah." My great uncle said it about his dog one time. He said, "She's as old as Methuselah." It wasn't until years later that I understood. Methuselah was the person with the longest earthly lifespan recorded in the Bible. He lived a total of 969 years. But that's not the interesting part. The name Methuselah means "when he is dead, it shall be sent." But we have to wonder what *it* is that will be sent? Biblical history tells us that *it* was the judgment upon the earth, meaning the flood.

It just so happens that when you subtract Methuselah's age at death with Noah's age at the time of the flood, it calculates out to show that Methuselah died the year of the flood. The fact that his very name meant "when he is dead, it shall be sent" shows his name was preordained by God as a final warning to the people living at that time. God is a God of judgment, but He is also a God of compassion who will use every means possible to save those who are willing to hear. Methuselah was the longest living human being recorded in the Bible. It is as if God had him live even longer than was normal at that time so every person who might possibly come to salvation could have ample opportunity and be without excuse. This reveals the heart of our God who is long-suffering, wanting none to perish but all to come to salvation. God waited beyond a normal human lifespan to show the fullness of His patience. One thing we can glean from this is that just because He is patient in withholding judgment doesn't mean He approves. May we never time out His patience.

Now let's back up to Methuselah's father, Enoch. Genesis 5:21–24 says, "When Enoch had lived 65 years, he fathered Methuselah. Enoch walked with God after he fathered Methuselah 300 years and had other sons and daughters. Thus, all the days of Enoch were 365 years. Enoch walked with God, and he was not, for God took him." The Bible doesn't say outright that God told Enoch to name his son Methuselah, but we can assume He did. How could Enoch possibly have known when the flood of judgment would come if God had not revealed it to him? It catches my attention that the Scripture says Enoch walked with God *after* he fathered Methuselah. It's as if God revealed to Enoch the name for his son Methuselah, which meant "when he is dead, it shall be sent," and Enoch heard the prophetic warning loud and clear and got his heart right with God. Only after Enoch fathered Methuselah did he walk with God.

Sometimes we have to have a wake-up call on our lives, don't we? Sometimes something so profound has to shake us awake. Sometimes it takes getting caught. Sometimes it takes getting tangled in sin for us to see it for what it is and to make us desperate for change. Sometimes it takes a circumstance to make us realize time is short and our lives need an adjustment to live for eternal things. Have you ever been shaken awake? Enoch was shaken awake, so much so that Jude 14–15 reveals that Enoch spent the rest of his life prophesying about the coming judgment.

Enoch is one of only two men recorded in the Bible who were taken by God to heaven alive and never died. Genesis 5:24 says, "Enoch walked with God, and he was not, for God took him." As I was writing this book, when I read that line, I paused instantly and wrote in my notes, "Enoch—why did God take him instead of death? There's something there."

One thing I've found through the years when studying Scripture is that God doesn't unnecessarily include details. Everything in the Word is there for a reason, so when some oddity comes up like this detail, there may be more to it, and we should start digging. Multiple scholars believe that the reason Enoch was taken alive to heaven instead of encountering death is because he was a picture of the New Testament rapture of the church before the final judgment. Just as God snatched up Enoch, we who are alive when Christ returns will be snatched up to meet Him in the air before the beginning of the final judgments upon the earth.

In light of this picture in your head, let's look at 1 Thessalonians 4:15–17:

> For this we declare to you by a word from the Lord, that we who are alive, who are left until the coming of the Lord, will not precede those who have fallen asleep. For the Lord Himself will descend from heaven with a cry of command, with the voice of an archangel, and with the sound of the trumpet of God. And the dead in Christ will rise first. Then we who are alive, who are left, will be caught up together with them in the clouds to meet the Lord in the air, and so we will always be with the Lord.

As Christ followers, if we are alive on the day of the rapture before the final judgment upon the earth, then we will be taken by God instead of by earthly death. Imagine that. We could be as Enoch who never faced death on the earth. Now *that* would be awesome.

Speaking of the rapture, did you know that the word rapture never actually occurs in the Bible? So where did we come up with this word that became so popular? Most of us heard it and immediately understood its meaning if we have ever read the Left Behind series by Tim LaHaye and Jerry B. Jenkins. But the word *rapture* was around before that. The concept of rapture came from a word in the passage we just read. Verse 17 says, "Then we who are alive, who are left, will be *caught up* [raptured] together with them in the clouds to meet the Lord in the air." The Bible wasn't originally written in English. The Old Testament was written almost entirely in Hebrew, and the New Testament was written almost entirely in Greek (though there was some Aramaic in both). Before the New Testament was translated into English, it was first translated from Greek into Latin. If you've ever studied etymology (the study of words and their origins and meanings throughout time), you'll find that a lot of our English words have Latin roots. Our English word *rapture* comes from the Latin word *rapio*, which means "to seize, snatch up, or be caught up." It was the Latin word *rapio* that was chosen when 1 Thessalonians 4:17 was first translated into Latin from Greek, but for clarity's sake, a more commonly known word is chosen from the definition and used in most Bible translations now instead of the more ancient word *rapture*. "Then we who are alive, who are left, will be caught up [*rapio* or *raptured*] together with them in the clouds to meet the Lord in the air."

When the Lord returns for us, He won't come all the way back down to earth. We will meet Him in the air, and He will take us to glory. But Jesus will eventually make His true second coming all the way back down to the ground of the earth. I will include a chart in this chapter later that will help you visualize our best guess based on Scripture of the order of end-times events. For now, just know that if you are a follower of Christ and He chooses to come back during our lifetime to rapture us, we get to identify with Enoch and be snatched up to heaven instead of facing death!

The Story of Noah: Did It Really Happen, or Is It Just Imagery?

I attended a week-long conference in Colorado Springs, Colorado, a few years ago. During one of the conference breaks, a few of us hiked up to view the rock formations in and around a place called The Garden of the Gods. The elevation is 6,400 feet above sea level. The rock formations showed evidence that the sea once stood high above the continent. There were fossilized imprints of creatures that only live in the oceans. There was evidence of a sudden worldwide shift in the earth's condition, and the unique formations replicated patterns that only deep, fast-moving water can form.

No other explanation besides a great, worldwide flood can more thoroughly explain these rock formations and ocean fossil imprints at such an elevation.

The Grand Canyon in Arizona also contains many scientific evidences to support a great and sudden worldwide flood. There's an interesting documentary called *Is Genesis History?*[10] that walks through the evidences in the Grand Canyon as well as sites all around the world. If you are one who doubts the Bible actually happened, you should consider watching this film.

I think it takes more theorizing to believe the flood *didn't* happen rather than to simply believe it did. Believing the worldwide flood did actually happen allows the evidence out there to naturally fall into place. I believe God is who He says He is. And I believe His Word is true and inspired. As time goes by more and more archaeological discoveries are uncovered and continue to support what the Bible has said to be true all along.

People bent on rejecting the Bible seem to have a hard time openly and unbiasedly considering evidence that supports Scripture. In a similar way I do this with my husband sometimes when we disagree. I get so bent on making sure I prove him wrong that I refuse to allow my mind to truly and openly consider his side. (I mean, I *am* always right, right?)

But, on the occasions that he is right, I can look back and see how my stubbornness kept me from being able to see his side. It is as if I am blinded by my own agenda during those kinds of debates. So, I know how easy it is to be blinded from truly considering the other side (especially if my heart has skin in the game), because I've done it before. But when it comes to eternal matters, it's just so hard to watch someone reject truth because they refuse to seek it unbiasedly. I am 100 percent convinced that Christianity is the truth. I've done the work to find truth. I am convinced by reputable historical documents, facts, science, the validity of Scripture, the logic of scholars, the evidence of my own heart coming alive, and my own life being transformed in Christ. But just for argument's sake, if Christians live their lives for Christ and are wrong, what do they lose? True Christians who are convinced of the gospel of the grace of Christ have purpose and hope. They aim to be good people who glorify God. They end up in most cases being good citizens who benefit the world, and they love and help the poor, downcast, and rejected find the hope that they themselves have found. No harm done. If people who reject Christianity are wrong, they lose everything because they reject the Word of God and Jesus, the only way to heaven according to the Bible. Lord, open eyes to see.

The Whole Picture

Okay, so if Enoch is a picture of the church being raptured before the end-times judgments, that means no believers remain on earth as a picture of what Noah would represent. So how does this picture hold true? We (Americanized Christians) so often forget about the Jewishness of the Bible. But if you let yourself forget that the Bible is the story of God's people Israel, out of which came Jesus our Messiah, and into which we (Gentiles) are grafted, then we will often misinterpret Scripture.

The Old Testament nation of Israel were God's people. They are also called Hebrews or Jews at certain points. The Old Testament follows the story of these people, allowing you and me to see not only our heritage but also the joys and mistakes and journeys of our ancestors with God. When we came to salvation in Christ, we were grafted into this family of people (see Romans 11). We get to be God's people, too, now because of Christ. He opened the door to all.

When Jesus came to earth in human form, most of the Jews living at that time rejected Him, even though He was the exact Messiah their Old Testament Scriptures pointed to. Jesus fulfilled every one of their messianic prophecies about his first coming, even down to tiny details such as in what city He would be born (Micah 5:2). But Jesus didn't do what the Jewish leaders thought He should do as a messiah, and He wasn't the messiah they were expecting Him to be.

In addition, they were threatened by Him. He often answered the "great" Jewish leaders' questions about the interpretation of God's law by pointing out the fact that even though they seemed to be following God's laws on the outside, their hearts and intents behind them were impure; and they were missing the reason for the laws in the first place. They needed a Savior Messiah who could change their hearts entirely, but they wouldn't see that. They believed they could attain holiness by their own adherence to the laws. They were offended by the truth, so they rejected Him.

Once the Jews rejected Jesus, the gospel began to be proclaimed to the Gentiles and, unlike the Jews, many of the Gentiles realized their need for a Savior. This shift marked the beginning the age of the Gentiles. Scholars sometimes call the time period we are living in right now the church age instead of the age of the Gentiles, since the church was birthed during this time. The entire chapter of Romans 11 talks more about the shift from Jew to Gentile and explains that Jews and Gentiles should appreciate each other because we have helped each other come to salvation and will continue to help each other come to salvation. It's an interesting mystery.

Romans 11:25–27 says, "Lest you be wise in your own sight, I do not want you to be unaware of this mystery, brothers: a partial hardening has come upon Israel, until the fullness of the Gentiles has come in. And in this way all Israel will be saved, as it is written, 'The Deliverer will come from Zion, he will banish ungodliness from Jacob; and this will be my covenant with them when I take away their sins.'"

In other words, the Jews have been partially hardened to accepting Christ for now. As Gentiles come to salvation, it will eventually end up making them jealous (Romans 11:11). The hardening will be lifted from them one day soon, and they will be refined in such an intense way (through the tribulation) that any stubbornness or ungodliness they may have will be gone from them forever.

Once believers on the earth are raptured, the church age (or the age of the Gentiles) will be over and the partial hardening of the Jews will be lifted. But if the rapture has already happened by this point, will it be too late for the remaining Jews to be saved? No. Not for the remnant of

Jews (and whatever Gentiles they convert during that time). However, since they did not come to salvation prior to the rapture of the church, they will have to endure seven years of tribulation (people call this the tribulation period, which includes the time of the ultimate Antichrist, warfare, famines, natural disasters, plagues, fire, and other judgments upon the world). The entire world that is left living at this time will have to endure it. Scripture says a Jewish remnant of 144,000 will be sealed for eternal salvation *before* any of the terrible judgments of the tribulation are unleashed. They will be sealed for eternal salvation, but they must still endure them—just like Noah. Noah was sealed for salvation from the start but still had to endure the flood of judgment within the safety in the ark. He didn't get snatched up like Enoch. He had to go through it but was sealed safe from eternal destruction.

It's interesting to note that Scripture says God Himself shut Noah and his family in the ark; it was God who closed the door to the ark. Similarly, in the end God will place a seal on the foreheads of the Jewish remnant to be saved through the tribulation. It is His seal that will save them, not their own efforts. When Jesus came, He declared, "I am the *door*. If anyone enters by Me, he will be saved" (John 10:9, italics mine). In the Noah story, Noah tried to preach to the people and get them to enter the ark with him, his family, and two of each animal. People called him crazy, dismissed him, and lived however they wanted, but in the end, it was only those who entered through the *door* of the ark that were saved. Similarly, Jesus, who called Himself "the door," is the only way for any of us to be saved from judgment.

After the flood of judgment upon the world was over, Noah emerged into a fresh, new earth. Likewise, on the other side of the tribulation and the total destruction of the current heaven and earth, the Jewish remnant will eventually emerge onto the soil of the new heaven, new earth, and new Jerusalem. Here's a chart to help you see the progression of the End Times a little better:

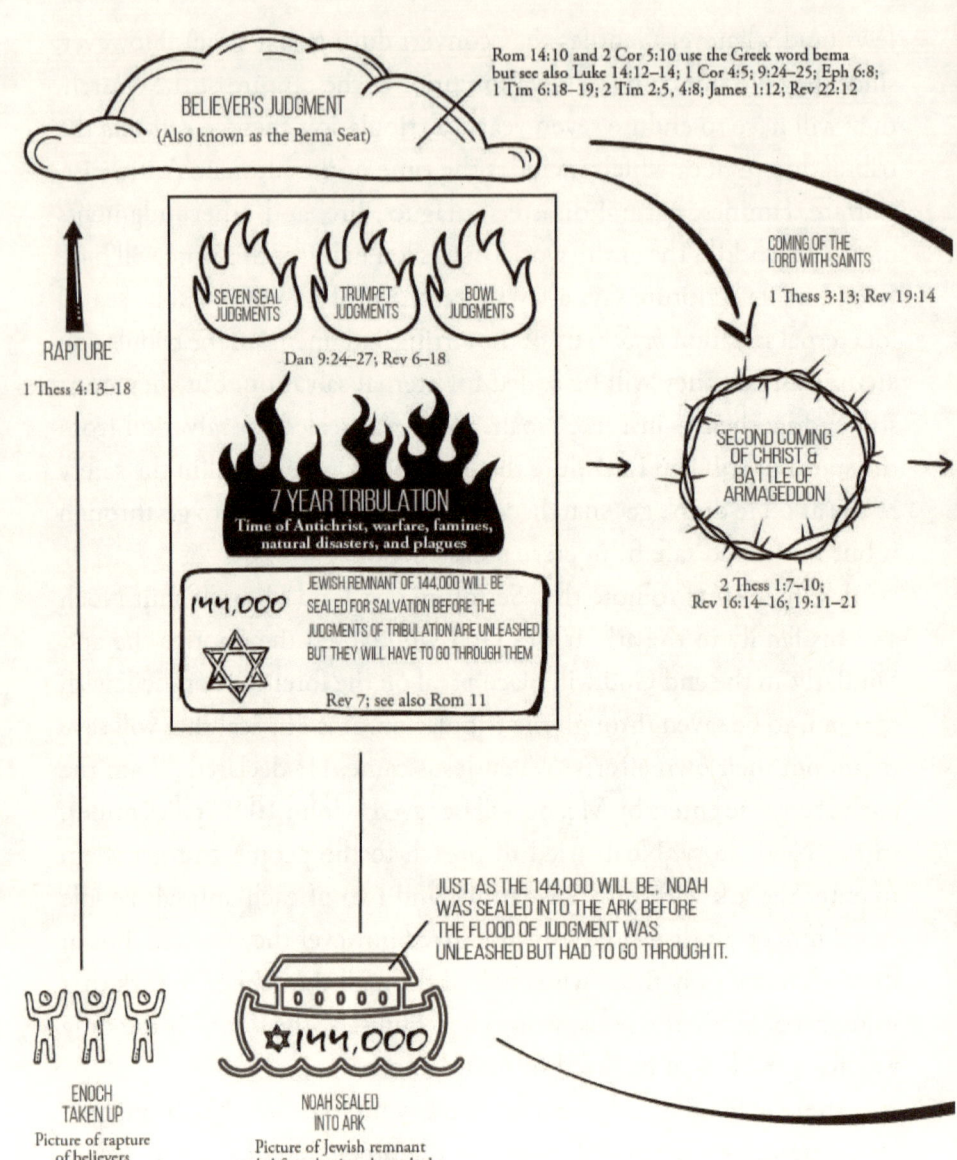

THE END TIMES (ENOCH, METHUSELAH & NOAH)

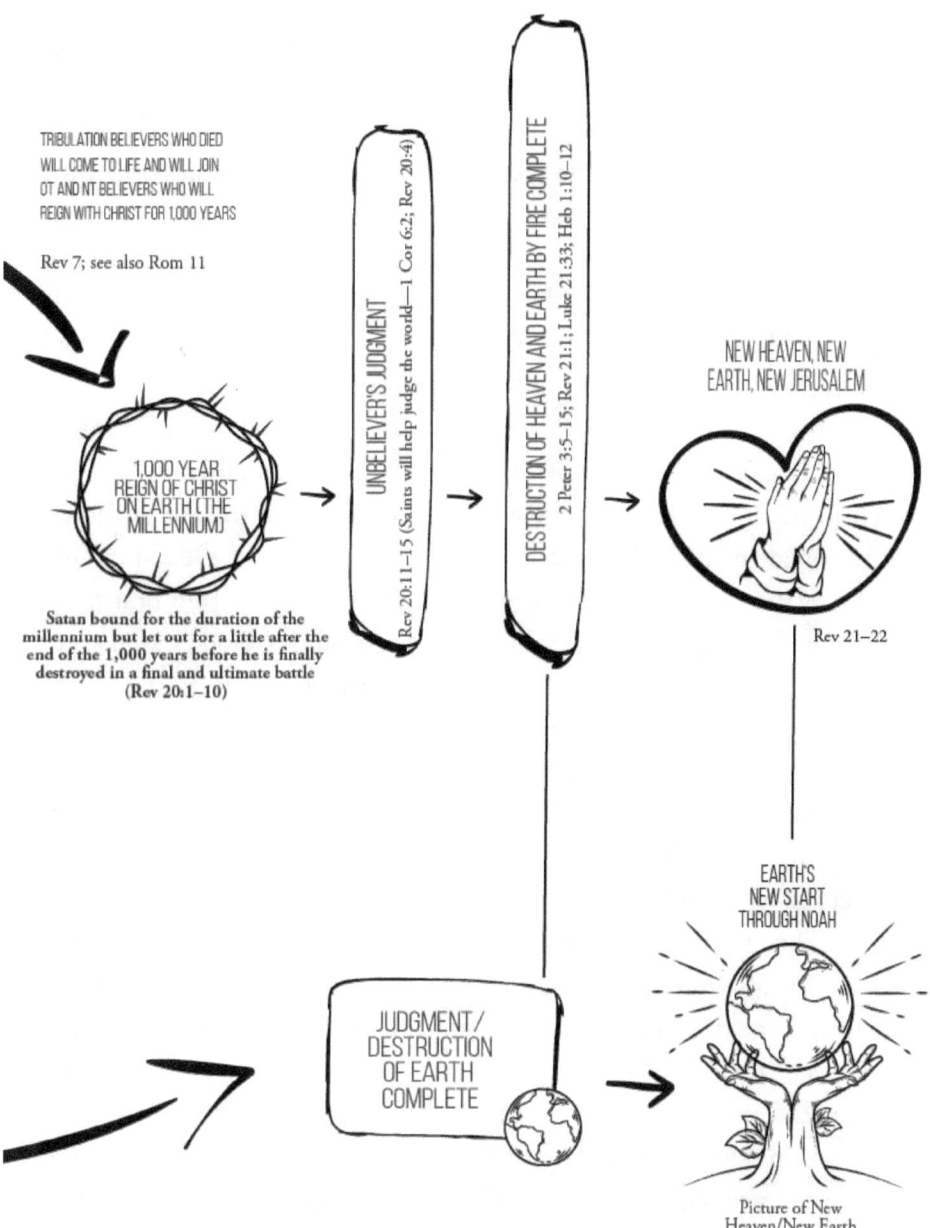

Picture of New Heaven/New Earth

Note: These are not all the Scripture references that exist on each topic. A study on each topic individually would prove beneficial. Please also note that this chart depicts the pretribulation rapture belief, of which I believe and find the most support for, but it could easily be modified to also support the midtribulation rapture belief. The midtribulation view works when we consider that the great tribulation doesn't begin until halfway through the seven-year tribulation period—the second half being the most intense of the tribulations by far.

The New Testament confirms this idea by referring to the End Times as being like the days of Noah. Concerning unbelievers and those hardened to the truth, Jesus Himself said, "For as were the days of Noah, so will be the coming of the Son of Man. For as in those days before the flood they were eating and drinking, marrying and giving in marriage, until the day when Noah entered the ark, and they were unaware until the flood came and swept them all away, so will be the coming of the Son of Man" (Matt. 24:37–39). The story of Enoch, Methuselah, and Noah is clearly a precursor to the rapture and final judgment.

After Noah emerged from the ark and made a burnt offering to God, God made a covenant with Noah, his descendants, and all the creatures of the earth that He would never again destroy the earth by a worldwide flood. This is also a picture of a promise to come. Once God creates the new heaven and new earth, He will never again destroy it. Period. Don't you love that? The reminder or sign of God's covenant to Noah, his descendants (us), and all the creatures of the earth was the rainbow. To Noah, seeing the rainbow reminded him that God would never again destroy the earth by a worldwide flood. And to this day we have had floods, but none have ever been worldwide, and none have destroyed the earth like it did that day. This shows the sovereignty of God over the wind and waves and God's commitment to keep His promise.

When we see the rainbow in the clouds today, we can remember that God was also foreshadowing the new heaven and the new earth, which He will one day make to replace this one, and we can look forward to the fact that He will never again destroy that new heaven or new earth. All will be as it should be forever. No sin, no evil, no sickness or sadness will be in that world; only the ones made righteous under the blood of Christ can enter, and we will all live forever together there face to face with Christ. There will be eternal peace and happiness. Let the rainbow in the clouds remind you of His faithfulness to us.

Because of God's covenant with Noah, the world cannot be destroyed by water again in the end. So how will it be destroyed in order to be replaced with the new earth? Second Peter 3:5–15 shows us that it will be destroyed by fire instead:

> For they deliberately overlook this fact, that the heavens existed long ago, and the earth was formed out of water and through water by the word of God, and that by means of these the world that then existed was deluged with water and perished. But by the same word the heavens and earth that now exist are stored up for fire, being kept until the day of judgment and destruction of the ungodly.
>
> But do not overlook this one fact, beloved, that with the Lord one day is as a thousand years, and a thousand years as one day. The Lord is not slow to fulfill his promise as some count slowness, but is patient toward you, not wishing that any should perish, but that all should reach repentance. But the day of the Lord will come like a thief, and then the heavens will pass away with a roar, and the heavenly bodies will be burned up and dissolved, and the earth and the works that are done on it will be exposed.
>
> Since all these things are thus to be dissolved, what sort of people ought you to be in lives of holiness and godliness, waiting for and hastening the coming of the day of God, because of which the heavens will be set on fire and dissolved, and the heavenly bodies will melt as they burn! But according to his promise we are waiting for new heavens and a new earth in which righteousness dwells.
>
> Therefore, beloved, since you are waiting for these, be diligent to be found by him without spot or blemish, and at peace. And count the patience of our Lord as salvation.

As you read that, did you notice the theme of patience that holds judgment back as long as possible—just like the extra-long lifespan of Methuselah whose name warned, "when he dies, it will come." I love the last line of the passage above: "And count the patience of our Lord as salvation." Sometimes I get downtrodden by this fallen world and desperately pray, *When are you coming, Lord? I'm not sure how much more I can take.* And then I remember the reason for God's long-suffering. If the Lord is still patient, then there are still souls that can be saved. He isn't willing to lose even one. As a believer because of what He has done for me, neither am I.

The Believer's Judgment

A lot of people get confused about what sort of judgment believers will go through after being raptured from this earth. People reason that if the blood of Jesus covers us and immediately makes the stain of our sin whiter than snow, how can we all of a sudden bear the terrible load of sin again in heaven at the time of judgment? They are absolutely correct. It would be a blood that couldn't fully be trusted in that case. But praise be to God, we can put our faith fully in the blood of Jesus once we have made Him Lord of our lives.

When Scripture talks about the believer's judgment, it says that we will gather at the "judgment seat of Christ." The judgment seat of Christ will be a place where rewards are given or lost depending on how one used their life for the Lord. It won't be a place of terrible, harsh punishment like the judgment unbelievers will have to face. The original Greek word for the judgment seat is *bema*. You might have heard people call the judgment seat of Christ the *bema* seat of Christ instead. Bible.org does a better job of explaining the original meaning of the *bema* seat by using the Greek culture to explain:

> This word is taken from Isthmian games (Olympic-type games) where the contestants would compete for the prize under the careful scrutiny of judges who would make sure that every rule of the contest was obeyed (cf. 2 Tim. 2:5). The victor of a given event, who had participated according to the rules, was led by the judge to the platform

called the *Bema*. There the laurel wreath was placed on his head as a symbol of victory (cf. 1 Cor. 9:24–25).

In all of these passages, "Paul was picturing the believer as a competitor in a spiritual contest. As the victorious Grecian athlete appeared before the *Bema* to receive his perishable award, so the Christian will appear before Christ's *Bema* to receive his imperishable award. The judge at the *Bema* bestowed rewards to the victors. *He did not whip the losers.*" We might add, neither did he sentence them to hard labor.

In other words, it was a reward seat and portrayed a time of rewards or loss of rewards following examination. It was not a time of punishment where believers are judged for their sins. Such would be inconsistent with the finished work of Christ on the cross because He totally paid the penalty for our sins.[11]

I don't know about you, but I'm super competitive. And since these are *eternal*, imperishable, and very valuable rewards, I want them all the more. Paul seemed to relish this concept because we can find hints of it in some of his other letters. Look at 1 Corinthians 9:24–26:

> Do you not know that in a race all the runners run, but only one receives the prize? So run that you may obtain it. Every athlete exercises self-control in all things. They do it to receive a perishable wreath, but we an imperishable. So I do not run aimlessly; I do not box as one beating the air. But I discipline my body and keep it under control, lest after preaching to others I myself should be disqualified.

Run the good race. Live the faith. Gain the prize.

A Better Adam and a Better Noah

Noah had been a man of great faith as the only righteous man left on the earth. He built the ark at God's command, endured the journey over the waters of the flood of judgment upon the earth, and came out of the ark on the other side. God made a covenant with him and gave him the sign of the rainbow, but then do you know what happened next? This great man of faith sinned in his new, fresh garden, just like Adam had done. Genesis 9:20–25 tells the main point of story. As you read, notice the similarities between Adam and Noah:

> Noah began to be a man of the soil, and he planted a vineyard. He drank of the wine and became drunk and lay uncovered in his tent. And Ham, the father of Canaan, saw the nakedness of his father and told his two brothers outside. Then Shem and Japheth took a garment, laid it on both their shoulders, and walked backward and covered the nakedness of their father. Their faces were turned backward, and they did not see their father's nakedness. When Noah awoke from his wine and knew what his youngest son had done to him, he said, "Cursed be Canaan; a servant of servants shall he be to his brothers."

What similarities did you see between the story of Adam and Noah? Both sinned. Both of their sins took place in a garden. Both of their sins led to shame and nakedness. Both men's nakedness had to be covered by someone else. And both men blamed their sin on someone else out of self-protecting pride.

The world started new with Adam in the garden. He screwed it up, and his descendants followed in his footsteps leading to the corruption of the world until the flood of judgment came. Then the world started over with Noah in a fresh, new garden. He got drunk and sinned and his descendants have followed in his footsteps corrupting the entire world. Today we are nearing a point of corruption when the rapture and judgment of the tribulation will come.

But here's the deal. Jesus is the one leading us in the new, fresh world this time. Unlike Adam and Noah, Jesus passed the garden test. Jesus passed the test in the garden of Gethsemane the night before

His crucifixion. The garden of Gethsemane is a garden of olive trees also known as the Mount of Olives. He passed the test in the garden of Gethsemane that night proving Himself to be a greater Adam and a greater Noah. He is worthy of leading us successfully in a new, fresh world and *keeping* it incorruptible forever. Therefore, we can trust that whatever garden might be in the new heaven or new earth, Jesus has already proven He can pass all garden tests.

He could have decided that night in the garden to disobey God and love his life more than obedience to God and choose not to die for our sins and save His own life. But He didn't. The test was so intense that Scripture says He was sweating blood. In anguish, He declared, "Father, if you are willing, remove this cup from me. Nevertheless, not my will, but Yours be done" (Luke 22:42). God did not remove the cup, and Jesus left there and was brutally put to death as our Lamb of God who takes our sins away. If He passed *that* garden test, He is qualified and can be trusted to lead spotlessly as our King in the garden of the new heaven and new earth. Jesus is the better Adam and the better Noah. In Him our hope is secure.

How do you live in your garden experiences in life? Rather than looking out for the good of others, do you choose self-comfort or self-protection? Do you blame others instead of fully owning what you do wrong? After you've confessed, do you allow yourself to be met with the fullness of grace that Jesus offers? Do you offer that same grace to others? If not, take some time to get with God and read Matthew 18:21–35.

CHAPTER 5

A Tale of Two Cities
(Nimrod's Tower of Babel)

CHARLES DICKENS IS FAMOUS for his book, *A Tale of Two Cities*. And, really, the Bible is a sort of tale of two cities as well. The first city is Jerusalem, the city of the living God and of Christ. The second is Babylon, the city of our Enemy—the father of the Antichrist. The Bible refers to these two main cities historically and symbolically throughout and allows them to play out side by side until the final battle that will come between the two symbolically in Revelation (Rev. 17–18). Both cities are woven throughout in all the genres of the Bible: historical accounts, prophetic writings, poetry, and letters.

Oddly enough, the opening sentence of Charles Dickens's *A Tale of Two Cities* portrays the stark contrast between our two biblical cities nicely (though it was not his intent):

> It was the best of times, it was the worst of times, it was the age of wisdom, it was the age of foolishness, it was the epoch of belief, it was the epoch of incredulity, it was the season of Light, it was the season

of Darkness, it was the spring of hope, it was the winter of despair, we had everything before us, we had nothing before us, we were all going direct to Heaven, we were all going direct the other way.[12]

The two cities in the Bible are as opposed to one another as Charles Dickens's opening line. We will want to be loyal to one and completely severed from the other.

In Scripture, literally and figuratively, Babylon is the image of corruption, idolatry, independence from God, pride, and rebellion. It opposes God, hates the people of God, and encourages temptations of the flesh and appetite. Babylon is called "the great prostitute" full of sexual immorality, demonic temptation, immorality, and the temptation to live luxuriously for oneself, growing rich and powerful (Rev. 17:1–2; 18:2–3).

In contrast to Babylon, "the great prostitute," the heavenly Jerusalem is described as a "bride adorned for her Husband" (Rev. 21:2). One is corrupt; one is pure. The new Jerusalem will come down from heaven to be the final and complete dwelling place of God and humanity (Rev. 21:2–3). For a more thorough and detailed contrast between the two, read Jeremiah 50–51 and Revelation 17–21.

Even today the world seems to be at the bidding of Babylon—maybe more than ever before. Idolatry (prioritizing anything or anyone above God), love of money, demonic curiosity, sexual obsession, temptations of the flesh, temptations of the appetite, pride, independence from God, luxurious living, and desiring power and riches. Temptation is aired across our TV screens, in our movies, on our laptops, in our conversations, on our iPhones, in our music, on our billboards, in the way we mission our lives, and in how we raise our kids. I'm not just talking about unbelievers; we as believers have been enticed and entangled in her schemes as well.

No one is immune; therefore, a total desperation for and total dependence on God to see us through is necessary. Babylon's pull is a powerful force that infiltrates our culture.

Speaking about these very temptations, Paul warns, "If you think you are standing firm, be careful that you don't fall! No temptation has overtaken you except what is common to mankind. And God is faithful; He will not let you be tempted beyond what you can bear. But when you are tempted, He will also provide a way out so that you can endure it" (1 Cor. 10:12–13 NIV). The minute we think we are immune, we let our guard down and we are vulnerable to the lures of Babylon. She starts small and "harmless" and gradually increases her corruption, callousing us over time to be okay with what used to shock us. That's why so many people who are caught in sin mournfully look back and say things like, "I never believed I would do that. I don't know how it happened." And once temptation and sin has you in her snares, she doesn't let go very easily. But God is our ever-present help if we will just call to Him when we start to get tangled. He is full of grace for those who cry out to Him (Heb. 4:16). He will provide a way out. The question is, will we call on Him for help? Or will we decide we don't really want help more than we want to indulge? I've been on both sides. I've asked for help and received it, but I've also stifled the prodding to ask for help and indulged. The latter has always brought destruction to my life. Always. But His help brings life. Always.

The Tower of Babel

The account of the Tower of Babel (Babylon) in Genesis 10–11 gives us real insight into the Enemy and his intentions for his city and the citizens of our world that he deceives into loyalty to him. The ruler of Babel (Babylon) was a man named Nimrod. Nimrod's very name means "the rebel,"[13] which is fitting since 2 Thessalonians 2:8–10 describes the Antichrist as "the lawless one."

Nimrod is a picture of the Antichrist who will rise up during the tribulation period (Rev. 12:7–13:18). The Antichrist will be powerful, deceitful, will be given authority, and will try to do the very same thing Nimrod tried to do with the tower of Babel. In the account of the Tower of Babel, Nimrod and his city no longer wanted to scatter and populate the whole world as God commanded. They wanted to stay in one place and build a tower so tall that it would make a name for themselves.

The worldwide flood wasn't long past, and no doubt the people feared that a flood could wipe them out again. It's possible that some of the people, enticed with sin and unwilling to give it up, probably feared judgment but loved their sin more. We can be the same today, can't we? So, the prospect of a leader who would fund and lead them to build a tower that would reach to the heavens was the immediate answer of security for the people of Babylon. With this plan for a tower, they could continue to live however they wanted and be immune to another flood of judgment, which was the only judgment from God they had known up to this point. They would make a name of power for themselves, and the whole world would flock to their tower because it would be tall enough that no flood could ever wipe them out again.

Even more intriguing is that the Tower of Babel is believed to have been a ziggurat, a pyramid-like structure with stairs almost to the top. Most ziggurats that have been uncovered in archaeological endeavors contained temples to various gods at the very top of them.[14] If that was the case with Nimrod's tower, no doubt the temple at the top was not associated with the correct God. In fact, early on, the translation of the word babel was "gate of God"—it wasn't until after the confusion of languages that babel came to mean "confusion."[15] So, this tower of the Enemy that would reach to the heavens and possibly harbor a temple with an image of a god at the top, and in a town that meant "gate of God," seems very formulated by Satan. Revelation 13:15 says the Antichrist will "cause those who would not worship the image of the beast to be slain." Satan *desires* to be worshipped as God in all the forms he takes. And, apparently to some degree, he was successful that day. The *Complete Bible Commentary* says that "Nimrod, after his death, was worshipped under many names. These names constantly appear in ancient history."[16] Nimrod's tower did, in fact, succeed in making him a name for himself. And Babylon did succeed in becoming a great enemy kingdom, literally and figuratively.

Languages

At the time of the building of the tower of Babel, the whole world spoke one language. God saw the tower they built and said,

> "Behold, they are one people, and they have all one language, and this is only the beginning of what they will do. And nothing that they propose to do will now be impossible for them. Come, let us go down and there confuse their language, so that they may not understand one another's speech." So, the Lord made them speak many different languages and scattered them over the face of the earth. (Genesis 11:1–9)

Some read this story and think God was threatened by them and feared they would overtake Him, and that's why He made many languages and scattered them. But God's concern was not for Himself, for He is all-powerful; His concern was likely for His remaining people on the earth. If Nimrod was acquiring a kingdom with a mass following and his following had no breakdown in communication and had one purpose to annihilate God and His people, God's people on earth would suffer greatly under their power. It was too early in the game for that. His people had to be preserved so Christ could come out of them. So it was out of mercy and protection for His people that God scattered the Enemy and his followers and made many languages—thus thwarting Satan's plan. Once again, during the great tribulation, Satan will push for this oneness of vision and rule, knowing how powerful it can be. The book of Revelation insinuates a type of one-world government, universal rule, and universal currency (Rev. 13:11–18). And he will overcome many at that time.

But the Holy Spirit given at Pentecost showed that the Tower of Babel curse of the confusion of language can be reversed as needed for God's kingdom purposes. At Pentecost God enabled His people to speak by the power of the Spirit in whatever language their listener needed. Acts 2:4–7 says,

> And they were all filled with the Holy Spirit and began to speak in other tongues as the Spirit gave them utterance. Now there were dwelling in Jerusalem Jews, devout men from very nation under heaven. And at this sound the multitude came together, and they were bewildered, because each one was hearing them speak in his own language. And they were amazed and astonished, saying, "Are not all these who are speaking Galileans?"

God is all-powerful, even over language.

One day, all of God's people will speak one language again in total unity. The prophet Zephaniah spoke of a post-tribulation future in which God restores one language to His people at last: "For at that time I will change the speech of the peoples to a pure speech, that all of them may call upon the name of the Lord and serve Him with one accord" (Zeph. 3:9). The curse will be reversed.

People debate about whether this account in Scripture is truly the source of our various languages today. Since I have become convinced that the Bible is inspired, true, and accurate, it's easy for me to say that the Tower of Babel was the source of our many languages on earth today. Truly it seems to be the clearest explanation that exists. However there are others who believe that all languages evolved over time from one. Of course, we know that *every* language evolves. We have seen that in our own English language. There's what we call Old English. If you've ever picked up a book written in Old English and tried to read it, it's difficult to decipher word meanings. So, yes, languages naturally evolve and always will. There are words being added and made obsolete from our dictionaries constantly. But entire sentence structures and rules of grammar don't change like that. That's the problem with the stance that says all languages evolved from one. What we find when we compare the different languages of the earth is a great diversity in the form of grammar. In order for the evolution of languages theory to be true, whole sentence structures and grammar rules would need to evolve immensely as well. We don't see that happening to that degree when you study languages over time. In my opinion, it takes more faith to believe that all languages evolved from one rather than to just believe that what God said in His Word is true. Kind of like the Big Bang Theory. Sometimes it takes more faith to believe the lie, and yet sadly so many do it willingly just to avoid believing God.

A Cursed Lineage

Fittingly, our Antichrist type, Nimrod, came from the cursed line of Noah. The end of the last chapter mentioned the curse that Noah issued to his son, Ham, and Ham's son, Canaan, because Ham had seen Noah's nakedness and didn't cover him but instead went and told the other brothers. In biblical times, if your father was a close follower of God and cursed you, it was a prophetic curse, meaning it was going to happen just as he said. And if your father blessed you, it was prophetic, and blessings would come. Noah had cursed Ham by cursing his son, Canaan, but Noah blessed Shem and Japheth. Yet Noah gave a superior blessing to Shem.

And, as it goes, Jesus came out of the specially blessed line of Shem. And Nimrod, a picture of the Antichrist to come, came from the cursed line of Ham. When you sort through the genealogies of the cursed lines of Ham and Canaan, you find that many of the enemies of Israel in biblical history and even today descended from those lines. See if you recognize any enemies of Israel out of these people groups and nations taken from the genealogies of Ham and Canaan in Genesis 10: Assyria (Syria), Nineveh (the wicked city Jonah later preaches to), Casluhim (from whom the Philistine enemies came), the Canaanites, Gaza (we hear of the Gaza strip in turmoil with Israel even today), Sodom, Gomorrah, Egypt, Cush. Do you see any you recognized from reading the Bible and listening to world news? It sounds like the curse spoken over those lines still has ripple effects even today.

It's no coincidence that Nimrod, "the rebel," comes from the cursed line of Ham. First, the Bible says Nimrod "was the first on earth to be a mighty man" (Genesis 10:8). Daniel 11 says the Antichrist will be a "king" who will "prosper till the indignation is accomplished" and "shall magnify himself above all" (vv. 36–37). Nimrod was a king; he prospered; and he was a "mighty" man whose main goal was to make a name for himself.

Second, the Bible says Nimrod "was a mighty hunter before the Lord" (Genesis 10:8–9). When this passage says Nimrod was a mighty hunter before the Lord, that's not a good thing. It's more a note of arrogance on his part because of how he hunted people and did it openly in front of the Lord. Scripture often says things are done "before the Lord" in order to reveal the arrogance, such as in Genesis 13:13, "But the men of Sodom were wicked and sinners before the Lord exceedingly." So, Nimrod was a hunter before the Lord, and most likely, people were full of terror when they encountered him because he slayed people in order to take over.

One piece of land wasn't enough for Nimrod. He wanted it all and wanted all people subject to him. According to *The Complete Bible Commentary*, "He was practically king of the whole earth."[17] Scripture says he had already conquered and acquired a kingdom for himself: "The beginning of [Nimrod's] kingdom was Babel, Erech, Accad, and

Calneh, in the land of Shinar. From that land he went into Assyria and built Nineveh, Rehoboth-ir, Calah, and Resen between Nineveh and Calah; that is the great city" (Gen. 10:10–12). Jesus described Satan as the "ruler of this world" (John 12:31). As born-again believers of Christ, we are not of this world ruled by Satan. We live as ambassadors of a kingdom not of this world but of the one to come. Unbelievers are living for the kingdom of Satan here and now, whether intentionally or unintentionally. They are deceived into believing that this world is as good as it gets, and it's this world they live for.

Every day people are consciously or subconsciously giving their allegiance to Satan and this temporary world. One thing Billy Graham used to say at some of his rallies was when you hear the truth about Christ, everyone makes a decision. Even if we don't check yes or no on a card or walk down the aisle or make a conscious decision for or against Christ, we are still making a decision. When you leave a conference (or a book in this case) and walk away thinking, "I don't want to make a decision right now," you're still making a decision. There's only one side or the other. As Jesus says in Revelation 3:16, "So, because you are lukewarm, and neither hot nor cold, I will spit you out of my mouth!" Lukewarm people meddle in the things of God *and* things of the world. Overall they appear to be good people, but their allegiance isn't solid.

Billy Graham shared an example at a conference. It went something like this. What if you were in a physical war and decided you weren't ready to make a decision about which side to fight for? If you put on the pants and hat of one side and the shirt of the opposing side, then you get shot by both sides!

With God, it's either hot or cold, for or against. I promise you, the kingdom of the Enemy is not the kingdom where you want to let your soul rest. The Enemy's kingdom is selfish, not selfless, and in the end won't be standing to look out for your good anyway. If you've never said yes to surrender your life totally to Christ, then there's no better time than today. Tomorrow is never promised. God is just a prayer away.

A Lesson for Us Today

Everything God does, Satan tries to create a counterfeit. God plans a kingdom for His people; and Satan builds one too. God is to be worshiped; Satan thinks he should be too. God sent Christ who performed signs and wonders, died for our sins, and was resurrected; and Revelation says the Antichrist will one day do signs and wonders to deceive many. Depending on interpretation of Revelation, the Antichrist may even supposedly "die" and then fake a resurrection in order to fool the people into believing him. Satan's version is always similar to God's but is corrupted and deceitful.

The people of Babylon built a physical tower that reached to the heavens, but Revelation 18:5 says it will one day be the people of Babylon's sins (unbeliever's sins) that are seen "heaped high as heaven." And yet the new Jerusalem will come down out of heaven from God to earth (Rev. 21:2). Note those two verses. In Satan's version, he starts from here and builds up. In God's version, He builds up there and brings it down to us.

Satan is the biggest copycat there is, but his antics bring deception and uncertainty, and that's the point. If he can get us to question everything we *know* to be true, he has won. Indecision is still a decision.

Think about the ways the Enemy attacks you personally. If you're like me, he probably uses fear and lies that are tied to your most vulnerable hurts and insecurities. He probably shames you into believing things about yourself that are contrary to what God says in His Word and has in mind for you.

After Jesus died for our sins and resurrected proving his power over sin and even death, a new epoch of time was ushered in. Because the blood of Jesus now covered and made righteous those who trusted in Him, God in His holiness could draw near. He sent His Spirit to dwell within believers, making us the new temple of God. We were given a new heart that would naturally desire to know Him more (Jer. 24:7). On that new heart He has written His laws and the conviction that we are His (Jer. 31:33). His Spirit and the new heart He has given us work from the inside to alter the outside (Ezek. 36:27). It's a process from the inside out. The inside is ever growing and changing for good or bad (hopefully good), depending on how much we allow the Spirit to draw near versus how much we quench Him.

But the idea is that the only way for true change to happen is from the inside out. Through the cumbersome laws of the Old Testament, God proved to us that we can't truly change when we are given laws to obey on the outside and asked to make our inside conform without His help. He had to change us from the inside out. After Jesus's payment for our sin, we get that opportunity. The moment we surrender our lives to Him, He gives us a new heart and sends His Spirit to dwell within us. We are born again as a new creation in Christ (2 Cor. 5:17; John 3:1–15). After we are born again, every time we read the Word, the Spirit weaves it into our hearts, stirring the sanctification process from the inside out.

Here's the problem. The Enemy knows about this shift under the new covenant that God made with us. So the Enemy also knows that a tactic of corrupting us from the outside will be less effective now that we have a new heart and God's Spirit inside us.

So, here's what I've discovered that the Enemy does with me. I realized this one day when I was jogging with my English Springer Spaniel, Briley. We live in the country, so he runs beside me without a leash. One day he ran off a little further into the woods than I was comfortable with, so I called him back to me. When he came out of the tree line, he had a freshly shed snakeskin in his mouth. Immediately I gave him the command to "leave it," and he dropped it on the ground. As I stopped to examine it (with my canine companion intently staring at it alongside me), I think I began to understand why the snake is associated with Satan in the Bible.

The similarities are intriguing. The snake has no hands or feet and operates by cunning and craftiness—in the case of our Enemy, this means mind games! He comes to us with a lie, hoping that it will penetrate our hearts with venom, just as the teeth of the snake penetrates our skin with venom, creating a pathway to the inside. Because the snake has seen how God works from the inside out, he knows if he can get the venom inside our heart, it will rot everything it touches. He knows he has to find a way to get to our heart. What better way than to speak to us about our most vulnerable and painful areas? If he can just get us to believe we are the lies he is speaking, or get us to believe we aren't even worthy enough with Jesus's blood to do what we were purposed to do for the kingdom of God, the venom is in. The only antivenom there is, is to become convinced of the truth again—the truth found in the Word of God is our weapon. Everything you need to know about yourself and how God views you in Christ is in the Word of God.

Our minds are connected to our hearts, and our hearts are connected to our actions. That's why the Bible is so outspoken about washing our thought life with the Word of God. If we keep our minds on the truth, it allows our heart to do its job without corruption, and the right actions follow. Here's what Paul says, "We destroy arguments and every lofty opinion raised against the knowledge of God, and take every thought captive to obey Christ" (2 Cor. 10:5). And Proverbs says, "Guard your heart above all else, for it determines the course of your life" (4:23 NLT). Guard your heart by guarding your mind from the Enemy's lies about your heart.

You can move forward with confidence because nothing is wrong with you. You aren't too weird or too broken to be used. Even though we're not perfect, we are perfectly designed for the work we are called to do and the love we are called to give. God's work will always be more than you can do on your own. But that's the beauty of a partnership with God. We connect and depend on Him, and He does Kingdom things that only He can do in and through us. Block out the Enemy and his lies. Believe the One True God—He loves you like crazy.

The Devil's Playground

Think about *how* you struggle when you fall prey to believing the Enemy's lies. Do your struggles follow a similar pattern each time? Maybe you tend toward binge-watching TV for weeks on end in order to drown out life. Maybe during the dark times you allow yourself to slide back into unhealthy, codependent relationships. Maybe you find yourself dabbling with drugs and alcohol when times get tough. Maybe you purposefully isolate yourself and emotionally self-protect so no one can hurt you again. Maybe you allow overeating to pacify the boredom, pain, or stress. After you've identified *how* you tend to struggle, go deeper. What's the root underneath that struggle? What is the real fear you're trying to ensure doesn't come true? What's the real need under the surface that's not being fulfilled?

The root will be somewhat different for everyone, but I truly believe that in some way or another, many of our roots reveal a fear of being alone, a fear of being unlovable, or a fear of not being good enough for people. The human species is a social species created for community with a core need to love and be loved. When this is missing from our lives, many of us look to unhealthy places and habits to satisfy the emptiness, fear, and pain. This is where the devil plays.

If he can get us to look to anything else to satisfy besides God, His Word, and a community that's pursuing God, he knows we will end up worshiping that pacifier for the temporary relief it brings. And we will eventually have an unhealthy idol we run to instead of Christ, His Word, and His people.

The battle of loneliness is real. In fact, several times I have heard our age termed as the "age of loneliness." Why do we arrange our lives in a way that leaves us alone when in reality we long for relationships? It's as if the devil has been steering the body of believers further and further away from the safety of the fold and away from the Shepherd. Does a wolf try to take down ten sheep at once in a fold? No. He paces back and forth assessing the situation, looking for the sheep that has wandered away and is out from under the safety of the fold. The devil knows if he can get us alone and away, we are like a lone sheep in the teeth of a ravenous wolf. Why do we experience failure or feel shame and immediately isolate and withdraw in our times of greatest weakness when we don't fare well being alone for long periods of time?

Our technology, advances, independence, and accomplishments are making isolation easier and easier. Think about today versus even thirty years ago. Thirty years ago, housing used to be much smaller. Bedrooms were often occupied by multiple family members. Yet today, in the real estate market, privacy fencing is highly desired by buyers within cities. A family of five seeks a five-bedroom house so everyone has their own space. And I've often seen people drive into their garage and shut the garage door before ever getting out of their car. People are valuing privacy more and more and getting to know their neighbors less and less.

Technology brings convenience and worldwide connection, but not without penalty. Many of us have almost entirely replaced face-to-face relationships with digital ones. I hear of more and more instances where people's deepest relationships are online with a person they have never actually met. We are all being drawn into a subtle form of hiding.

In addition, businesses carefully study consumers and are aware of this shift toward isolation. There's e-counseling, online dating, online Bible studies, online music lessons, online churches, texting, Skyping, Voxing, Face Timing, social media, and the list goes on; each one was intended as a social *aid*. But instead, each one is being used to slowly *replace* face-to-face relationships.

A large number of young people suffer from social anxiety—maybe because although they feel well equipped to navigate through digital friendships, many feel much less equipped to know what to do with face-to-face relationships without technology. Do we even know *how* to have a healthy, close, non-digital community of relationships in our lives?

Christ and the support of other believers is the security wall that keeps the Enemy from being able to wreak havoc. When that security wall is weak or nonexistent, the Enemy tends to sneak in with tempting bait to lure us to lonely, destructive places that will ensnare us.

I recently read an article by Johann Hari called, "The Likely Cause of Addiction Has Been Discovered, and It's Not What You Think." This article was an extract from Johann Hari's book called *Chasing the Scream*. You might not struggle with drug or alcohol addiction and think what I'm about to share doesn't apply to you. However, I think we can all relate in our own way. Our "drug" might look different, but the concept is the same. In the article, Mr. Hari explained his research.

During the 1980s, The Partnership for a Drug-Free America advertised about an experiment showing the dangers of being addicted to heroin. In the experiment, a rat was put in a cage by itself and given two water bottles. One bottle contained fresh water; the other bottle contained water mixed with heroin. Almost without exception, each time they ran the experiment the rat would test both bottles but become obsessed with the drugged water. The rat would return again and again to the heroin-infested water until eventually it killed itself from overdose. Based on that experiment, heroin was deemed highly addictive and dangerous.

But in the 1970s, Bruce Alexander, a professor of psychology in Vancouver, began to think something was strange about this experiment. By nature rats are social creatures, and yet the experiment took the rat away from its life of community and isolated it in a cage so that it had nothing to do but to feel lonely and become obsessed with a drug that would pacify the ache of a life that didn't feel right.

Professor Alexander began to wonder if the experiment would have different results if the rats that were used in the experiment were offered a life-giving community with other rats. So, he built a rat park. The rat park was complete with tunnels, lots of rat-friends, food, and the same two water bottles used in the original experiment—one water bottle with fresh water and the other bottle drugged with heroin.

The rats tried both water bottles, not knowing what was in them. But what Dr. Alexander saw next was remarkable. The rats in this experiment did not prefer the drugged water. They mostly shunned it, and none of them died.

Thus, Dr. Alexander made the case that human beings, who were created for connection, are the same. For instance, when a person goes to the hospital with a broken hip or has to have surgery that requires pain medication, they are often given diamorphine, the medical name for heroin. Some patients take this medication for long periods of time for pain relief through the healing process. Interestingly enough, the heroin given by doctors has a much higher potency than the heroin drug dealers sell on the streets. Therefore, if the danger of addiction was entirely tied up in the drug itself, there would be tons of people who would recover from their ailment or medical procedure and go immediately to the streets to continue to feed their newly formed addiction.

But as Johann Hari discovered in his research, this almost never happens. Medical patients are almost entirely unaffected, while street addicts become desperate for more. The street addict is often like the rat in the first experiment, isolated and alone, with mainly drugs to turn to for comfort, while the medical patients are like the rats in the rat park community experiment, who go from the hospital back to a life where they are surrounded by a healthy, life-giving community of connection.[18]

The One who created us made us to be wired for connection. In fact, when Adam was alone God declared, "It is not good for the man to be alone" (Gen. 2:18). So it's no coincidence the New Testament Bible encourages us toward love and connection:

- Stay connected to the body of Christ. (1 Cor. 12:14–27)
- Don't forsake meeting together. (Heb. 10:24–25)
- Let only one debt remain: the continuing debt to love one another. (Rom. 13:8)
- Love the Lord your God with all your heart, soul, mind, and strength, and love your neighbor as yourself. (Matt. 22:36–40)
- Encourage one another as long as it is called today so that none of you will be hardened by the deceitfulness of sin. (Heb. 3:13)
- (Jesus's prayer for us) I pray for those that will believe in Me, that they may all be one as You and I are one, and that they also may be in us. (John 17:20–21)

If people don't connect with God and His body of believers, they will connect with something, whether it be a drug, a game console, a shopping addiction, a stranger on the other side of the screen—you fill in the blank. Author Johann Hari says, "The opposite of addiction is not sobriety. It is human connection."[19]

We all feel loneliness from time to time, even when connected to God and a healthy, growing community of believers. Loneliness never becomes entirely nonexistent from all moments this side of heaven. But the difference is, when we have God and a healthy dose of His people around us, the moments of loneliness can serve us well and become a tool to drive us deeper into Christ. It's the hard times that remind us we're not home, and they are necessary to refine us. It's often in the times of solitude that God chooses to speak most profoundly. But if we let the hard times and the times of solitude lead to chronic isolation, that's when the emotional, psychological, and moral trouble often begins.

Church people aren't perfect. They're messy. They have issues. But you and I do too. No matter what sort of group we commit to, if it is made up of people, it can get messy. Families are messy. Workplaces are messy. The church is messy. People are uniquely different at all stages of maturity, and anywhere a varied group like that decides to do life together, it will be messy at times. But with God's people, it will eventually be worth it. God's true people are our people—our eternal family—our support. So stick it out. Endure. Commit. Bear with one another—because God asks us to, and He knows what He's doing. We are part of each other's intended journey.

Hebrews 10:24–25

"And let us consider how to stir up one another in love and good works, not neglecting to meet together, as is the habit of some, but encouraging one another, and all the more as you see the Day drawing near."

CHAPTER 6

Everlasting Promises
(Abraham)

WHEN YOU THINK OF the nation of Israel, what comes to mind? Most people recognize Israel has ties to the Bible but aren't sure what to make of the modern Israel we know today. Most of us think of Israel as a tiny country in the Middle East that's constantly the center of hot debate and turmoil. During election years, many have prioritized a nominee for the President of the United States who has a "pro-Israel" stance. Perhaps you've wondered why this is even important to individuals in the United States.

Israel is a peculiar nation. Although it's small, it has had a great global impact. Interestingly enough, the following inventions originated in Israel: cell phone technology, voicemail technology, Amazon's Kindle, PlayStation, the first USB flash drive, the first instant messaging system, two of Microsoft's most popular operating systems for their computers (XP and NT), drip irrigation, the world's leading desalinization system (the process of turning salty sea water into clean drinking water), and the PillCam (a pill with a tiny camera that you swallow so doctors can easily detect disorders inside the GI tract).[20] And those are just a handful of the inventions brought to us by Israel.

When my husband and I traveled to Israel, we visited The Friends of Zion Museum. Instead of reading a chart or an informational plaque about each historical Jewish figure as would be typical at a normal museum, a hologram of the person spoke to us about his or her own life. It was incredible. I found myself swishing my hand through the image just to see if the figure would say "Ouch."

The vast amounts of technology that have come from such a tiny country is amazing. But where does such a small yet remarkable country have its roots? So far in our journey through Genesis, we've explored Adam and Eve, Abel, Enoch, Methuselah, and Noah—all of these people were followers of God, and yet up to this point there has been no mention of Israel. It's not until Abraham came on the scene in the Bible that God started building a foundation for a nation to call His own.

Abraham was the first man with whom God made a covenant to establish his own nation of people. God promised Abraham that through him would come a great number of offspring, a great name, and eventually a land to call their own (the promised land, Canaan)—all the makings of a nation.

If you're familiar with the Bible, the phrase "the God of Abraham, Isaac, and Jacob" probably has a familiar ring to it. God is referred to as the "God of Abraham, Isaac, and Jacob" approximately a dozen times in the Bible. These three people are the most widely known patriarchs of our faith. When God eventually changed Jacob's name to "Israel," this became the name by which all of Jacob's descendants became known as a whole. So, the people who descended from Jacob (Israel), his grandfather, Isaac, and his great-grandfather, Abraham, became known simply as "Israel."

It's easy to read something like this and think, *But hang on. I'm neither an Israeli, nor a Hebrew or a Jew, nor a follower of Judaism. I'm a*

Christian. How, then, do these three become fathers of my faith? These are the patriarchs of Jews and Judaism.

The Bible is made up of two main sections: the Old Testament writings and the New Testament writings. The Jews of Judaism hold to the Old Testament but reject the New Testament since they do *not* believe Jesus was their long-awaited Messiah. They're still waiting for another Messiah.

Jesus fulfills their Old Testament prophecies that describe the Messiah they should expect, but Jesus didn't come in the way they wanted so they rejected Him. They wanted their Messiah to come as a king and a military force who would immediately smite their enemies. But Christ didn't come that way for His first coming. He came as a Lamb during His first coming to die as a sacrifice for His people, but at His final coming, He will come like that, as a roaring Lion to take down the enemies of His people. The Jews ignored or misinterpreted the prophecies about His sacrifice and were looking for the Lion during His first coming instead of the Lamb, so they rejected Him and decided to wait for another.

If you're skeptical about Jesus being the one person who fulfills Old Testament prophecy, this is for you. A study by Professor of Mathematics Peter Stoner and his student mathematicians explored the probability of someone fulfilling the number of prophecies Jesus did. For the sake of simplifying the mathematical calculation, they decided to calculate the odds of Jesus fulfilling *only eight* of the sixty-one specific Messianic prophecies in the Old Testament that Jesus fulfilled. Keep in mind, Jesus fulfilled all sixty-one of the detailed prophecies about His first coming, and many of the them have no possibility of being controlled by one person in one lifetime. That speaks volumes toward divine fulfillment.

Here's what they found in their study: The odds are vastly against someone even fulfilling eight of the prophecies of the Old Testament. The odds of someone fulfilling eight of the chosen prophecies are one in ten to the 21st power (10^{21}). To give real-life application to that number, Professor Stoner gave the following example:

> First, blanket the entire Earth land mass with silver dollars 120 feet high. Second, specially mark one of those dollars and randomly bury it. Third, ask a person to travel the Earth and select the marked dollar, while blindfolded, from the trillions of other dollars.[21]

Not only that, but the eight Old Testament prophecies used in this study were written by different authors between five hundred to one thousand years before Jesus was born. This statistical scenario is for eight of the prophecies. The odds of Jesus fulfilling all sixty-one specific prophecies (and He does), would be beyond all mathematical possibility. For more information on this subject, pick up a book by Josh McDowell called *The Evidence that Demands a Verdict*.[22]

But, as we've said, many Jews simply refused to accept Jesus. So the question among the religious became, "How will we differentiate between the ones who believe Jesus *is* the promised Messiah and the ones who do *not* believe Jesus is the promised Messiah?" There was a fork in the road that called for redefinition. They decided that one road would continue to be known as Judaism and the other road would become known as Christianity. The group who did *not* accept Jesus continued in the ways of Judaism, religiously abiding by the Old Testament Mosaic law as best they could. But the ones who saw Jesus as the One the Old Testament Scriptures pointed to began to be called Christians. This new name was a play on "Jesus Christ." Christ means "Messiah," and Messiah means "the Anointed One." Contrary to what some may misunderstand, "Christ" wasn't Jesus's last name. When people said "Jesus Christ," they were actually saying, "Jesus, the long-awaited Messiah." They were proclaiming Jesus as the Anointed One promised long ago who would save us. "Christian" was a fitting name since it designated the new branch of Judaism whose followers believed their Messiah had come.

These new Christians, empowered by the indwelling of the Holy Spirit that Jesus sent after He resurrected, began to have a huge impact on the world—an impact that has never died.

Is there hope for the Jews who still do not believe in Jesus today? Are they still God's chosen people? Yes, God still has His eye on them. And there is prophecy in the Bible that indicates that a Jewish "remnant" will return to the Lord in the end times. They will accept Jesus and come to salvation. So there are at least a good number who will return. We should pray for them to come.

Judaism, Islam, and Christianity are still the three main religions in existence today, and, as we will see, all three of them got their start in the Old Testament. The lines of Judaism and Christianity hold to the bloodlines of Abraham, Isaac, and Jacob that lead to Jesus, whereas the religion of Islam claims the bloodline of Abraham through Ishmael, not Isaac (more on this in a couple of chapters).

If you're a Gentile (non-Jew) like me, then you might feel a sense of separation from your spiritual heritage since it's Jewish. But don't, because Galatians 3:29 says, "And if you are Christ's, then you are Abraham's offspring, heirs according to promise." And Romans 9:4–8 says (italics mine),

> They are Israelites, and to them belong the adoption, the glory, the covenants, the giving of the law, the worship, and the promises. To them belong the patriarchs, and from their race, according to the flesh, is the Christ, who is God over all, blessed forever. Amen. But it is not as though the Word of God has failed. *For not all who are descended from Israel belong to Israel, and not all are children of Abraham because they are his offspring, but "Through Isaac shall your offspring be named." This means that it is not the children of flesh who are the children of God, but the children of the promise are counted as offspring.*

My friend, if you have put your trust in Christ, you are one of the children of the promise. We are spiritual offspring of Abraham, Isaac, and Jacob because the blood of Christ claimed us and allowed us to be grafted into God's people. There's a spiritual Israel and a physical Israel, which are distinct in the Bible—even the promises are different for each as we will see in this chapter. We don't become the physical Israel or own all the promises given to the physical Israel, but since we are grafted in as the spiritual Israel, we can know we are God's children too.

No Merit

When we think of the people in the Bible, isn't it easy to assume they were better than us? More worthy, maybe? Had a better head on their shoulders? Were more gifted? Well, it's actually not true. The more I study Scripture, the more I find that the biblical characters were only noteworthy because of the work God did through them. You and I will only be noteworthy because of the work God does in us and through us too. Everything good in us is from God and belongs to God. He gifts us with life and abilities and ordains the times and places where we live (Acts 17:26). We only ever become anything good because of Him, whether we are conscious of that or not. "For it is God who works in you, both to will and to work for his good pleasure" (Phil. 2:13). We didn't even do anything significant to initiate our salvation in Christ. As we will see, neither did Abraham.

Jesus Himself said, "You did not choose me, I chose you" (John 15:16). Jesus also said, "All the Father gives me *will* come to me, and whoever comes to me I will never cast out" (John 6:37, italics mine). Paul said, "For he says to Moses, 'I will have mercy on whom I have mercy, and I will have compassion on whom I have compassion.' So then it depends not on human will or exertion, but on God, who has mercy" (Rom. 9:15–16). James 1:18 says, "Of His own will He brought us forth by the word of truth, that we should be a kind of first fruits of his creatures."

These verses speak to the fact that salvation is initiated by God, not by us. We only respond or not. He is the Great Pursuer. Or as the profound poem says, He is the "Hound of Heaven"—tracking us down, like a hound dog ever intent on pursuing its game until it's caught. The modern version of the Hound of Heaven portrays the idea that God stirs our hearts with a deep yearning in order to draw us to Himself. We often don't understand our yearnings and try to fill them with things that don't fit the God-sized hole that actually causes them. This causes problems. The poet notes, "The more I fed my desires, the more they consumed me."[23] The things the poet turned to in order to pacify his God-sized hole didn't love him well, and they eventually all fell away. So, in the end, the great Hound of Heaven and the poet dialogued. The poet explained, "I had no flight left, so I finally listened, 'Which of those you fled to loved you?' I heard him say. And my heart answered: 'None but you, only you.'"[24]

We don't orchestrate our own salvation. If we come to salvation, it's because He stirred our hearts and we responded. If we reject Him, we do so willingly and are without excuse. Someone once asked me, "But what about the people who never hear the gospel? How can they be found at fault?" In God's sovereignty, I believe He stirs their hearts to the existence of a Creator at some point in a way that they know. Romans 1:20 says, "From the creation of the world God's invisible qualities—His eternal power and divine nature—have been clearly seen, being understood from what has been made, so that people are without excuse" (NIV). The creation itself is a testament to the existence of a Creator. This is why people, even in remote villages with no human contact, have religion. There's something written in us that knows it should look to One greater than us.

There's a book by Tom Doyle called *Dreams and Visions: Is Jesus Awakening the Muslim World?* This book speaks to the personal way God pursues people. Tom Doyle and his wife are missionaries in the Middle

East and surrounding areas. In recent years missionaries have seen a drastic spike in the number of Muslims who have come to salvation in Christ. Doyle's book tells salvation story after salvation story. Often a Muslim man or woman will start having dreams about a man dressed in white. They describe the man in their dreams precisely as Jesus is described in the transfiguration account and Revelation. The dreams are detailed and feel so real that they stick firmly in their minds and hearts. They often have the dreams over and over. When Tom and his team show up and share Scripture about who Jesus is and what He has done, a certain feature or characteristic will trigger from their dream and they enthusiastically start saying, "That's the man who's been coming to me in my dreams! He even told me that someone would come and tell me about him!"

When a Muslim makes a decision to become a Christian, it can be very dangerous and heart-wrenching. They are often killed or cast out from their family and friends for converting to Christianity. But since Jesus has showed up to them in dreams and visions, by the time the missionary says the name Jesus their hearts have already been opened to considering or accepting the One who cares enough to pursue them so personally. They are willing to die for this Jesus who loves them so much. I can't even type that without tears in my eyes. Oh the ever-pursuing love of God!

Make no mistake, God pursues us first. We just respond one way or another. We have no merit in it because He is the catalyst. But the fun thing is that after we are saved, He asks us to partner with Him in the pursuit of others. His heart longs for all to come to salvation. "The Lord is not slow to fulfill His promise as some count slowness, but is patient toward you, not wishing that any should perish, but that all should reach repentance" (2 Pet. 3:9). He often gives chance after chance; you just can't know when it is the last chance. Don't miss it.

Abraham had no merit in his salvation either. In fact, later in the Bible, it is revealed that Abraham's family was actually serving other gods when the Lord called Abraham out from among them:

> Thus says the Lord, the God of Israel, "Long ago, your fathers lived beyond the Euphrates, Terah, the father of Abraham and of Nahor; and they served other gods. Then I took your father Abraham from beyond the River and led him through all the land of Canaan, and made his offspring many." (Josh. 24:2–3)

There is no reason dependent upon Abraham that God chose Abraham over his brothers or other men on earth. Let that sink in for you personally. There is no reason dependent upon you that God chose you. But if He chose you, you are one of the elect. You are His. You are called and loved. The Hound of Heaven has sought you out. The gratitude that fills my heart when I think it could have been the other way is overwhelming. I'm so thankful He chose me and so many of you.

Gratitude brings a lot of benefits mentally and psychologically—more than I think science has even discovered. So, get to the place today where the gratitude in your prayers runs deep for Christ. Make it fresh and sincere. "In everything give thanks; for this is the will of God in Christ Jesus concerning you" (1 Thess. 5:18 KJV).

Surrender and Promise

When God called Abraham out from among the pagans, He didn't ask for a halfhearted follow, He asked for total surrender. God initially asked three things of Abraham: (1) leave your country, (2) leave your kindred and your father's house, and (3) go to the land I will show you (Gen. 12:1). In other words, surrendering to the call of God often shakes up our premade plans and requires some hard changes.

When any believer comes to true salvation in Christ, he or she is asked for a deep, life-altering commitment of surrender. In the Bible, we never really see Jesus begging people to follow Him. Perhaps you've had experiences where you've heard people presenting Christianity as flowers and butterflies or the path to success and pleading with the audience to come to salvation. While the intention of their hearts may be good, the truth is, the Bible asks us to count the *cost* of following Christ before we make the decision.

In Luke 14:28–30, Jesus gives the people an illustration about first counting the cost of following Him. He asks them to liken accepting Christ to accepting a project to build a tower. He asked them if when a person decides to build a tower, doesn't he or she first sit down and estimate the amount of money it will take to build it? If a person were to lay the foundation but never finish it, people would ridicule and point out that he or she had started but weren't able to finish. If we lay the foundation of Christ and say we have given our lives to Him but don't follow through for the rest of our lives, our witness will actually do a disservice to Christ.

One of my friends recently had a conversation with a woman on a plane. The woman on the plane said, "I watched Christians for a long time before I decided whether I wanted to be one or not." Thankfully the woman had assessed and decided to become a Christian, but what if she had seen Christians who had a foundation in Christ but never followed through in a life for Christ? She might not have made the same decision.

Luke 9:57–62 records some interactions between Jesus and those who wanted to follow Him. Notice that Jesus didn't beg anyone to follow. The cost is high. The decision is life-altering.

> As they were going along the road someone said to Him, "I will follow You wherever You go." And Jesus said to him, "Foxes have holes, and birds of the air have nests, but the Son of Man has nowhere to lay His head." To another He said, "Follow Me." But he said, "Lord, let me first go and bury my father." And Jesus said to him, "Leave the dead to bury their own dead. But as for you, go and proclaim the kingdom

of God." Yet another said, "I will follow You, Lord, but first let me say farewell to those at my home." Jesus said to him, "No one who puts his hand to the plow and looks back is fit for the kingdom of God."

Following God often takes painful surrender of our so called "rights" in this temporal world, but remember that God doesn't call us and ask us for surrender without also offering His faithfulness, promises, and eternal salvation to us in exchange. There are many promises in Scripture for believers. There were promises for Abraham as he answered the call as well. God commanded three things of Abraham when He called him, but He also issued his covenant (promise) in return. Here are the initial promises God gave him: "I will make of you a great nation, and I will bless you and make your name great, so that you will be a blessing. I will bless those who bless you, and him who dishonors you I will curse, and in you all the families of the earth shall be blessed" (Gen. 12:2–3). These everlasting promises still stand today. Let's dig a little deeper into each one:

Everlasting Covenant Promise 1: I Will Make of You a Great Nation

As we all know, God has made from Abraham a great spiritual nation of believers (us), but Israel is also a great physical nation. Though one of the smallest of the world's 194 countries, it currently ranks 8 (at the time of this writing) in the world's most powerfully influential countries—a tiny footprint that makes a huge impact on the world.[25]

Israel ranks as one of the most educated and has one of the most powerful militaries in the world, and, as we have already discussed, leading technology and inventions continue to come from Israel. Additionally, Israel and America have a great partnership. Strategically, Israel is an important ally for America to have in many ways, but especially in the war on terrorism and Islamic extremism. Israel gives America important intel using their state-of-the-art technology, and America has helped Israel militarily and financially in times of need as well. After the holocaust, it was realized that the Jews needed a place to call their own. There seemed no better place than their biblical homeland. So, in 1948, Israel became the only Jewish state and has grown and prospered ever since. America has always stood with Israel, even at times when Israel had no other friend.

Israel is a remarkable country with a huge influence, yet the entire country (today's borders) can be crossed by plane in a matter of minutes. In fact, I recently visited Israel and our tour guide told us that the Israeli Defense Force (IDF) has pilots sitting in fighter jets around the clock. They have their pilots take shifts in the cockpits. Since the country is too small to allow time for their pilots to travel to their planes in the case of enemy invasion, this is the only way they can be ready for air defense in time. The country of Israel today is *that* small. For a country so small to be on the top-ranking lists with the big boys is a big deal. Even if the physical Israel consists of people who have rejected God's Son as the promised Messiah, God's everlasting covenant promise to the Jewish Abraham still stands regardless. Second Timothy 2:13 says, "If we are faithless, he remains faithful, for He cannot deny Himself." In other words, faithful is who He is. To not be faithful to His promise to Abraham would be to deny Himself.

Everlasting Covenant Promise 2: I Will Bless You and Make Your Name Great So You Will Be a Blessing

This specific promise says, "I will bless you . . . so that you will be a blessing." Isn't that simple yet profound? If God blesses us, it is not so we can luxuriously live in our blessings or hoard our gifts to ourselves or use our blessings for our own glory. He blesses us *so* we will be a blessing. God has blessed Abraham and his physical descendants, and the promise still continues today for them. If you're ever curious, research inventions the Jewish people have brought into our world. I only selected a handful to mention earlier in this chapter. Some of the very things we take for granted today were invented by the God-blessed mind of the Jews.

As if that were not enough, God's promise to bless this people and make them a blessing to the world also shows in the history of Nobel Prize winners:

> As of 2017, Nobel Prizes have been awarded to 892 individuals, of whom 201 or 22.5% were Jews, although the total Jewish population comprises less than 0.2% of the world's population. This means the percentage of Jewish Nobel laureates is at least 112.5 times or 11,250% above average. Various theories have been made to explain this phenomenon, which has received considerable attention.[26]

They say "phenomenon"; I say the promises of God! The Jews are a people small in number, but they are blessed and are a blessing to the world whether they intend to be or not. Now, imagine a Jew who finds Christ to be the Messiah. *That* is a powerful combination—an already blessed people walking in the power of Jesus for the glory of God. Pray for the Jews to see Jesus for who He is. The dream in my heart is that one day Jews and Gentiles would fully unite together in Christ to glorify God. That would be breathtaking.

I don't know if you noticed, but we left out one piece of God's promise. I wanted to save it until now. It's the part of the promise where God says to Abraham, "I will . . . make your name great." The previous chapter in the Bible (and the previous chapter in this book) talked about the Tower of Babel and how the people were going to build a tower to the heavens to make a *name for themselves*, but God confused their language and scattered them. It's as if God, through his divine covenant with Abraham, was hammering in the idea that "everyone who exalts himself will be humbled, and he who humbles himself will be exalted" (Luke 14:11). It's as if God was playing on the Enemy's recent goal to have people make a name *for themselves* higher than God's. God didn't allow them to succeed, but He is fully capable of making a *great name* for the ones He chooses. At the Tower of Babel, people were trying to make their own names great. In the promise to Abraham, God says *He* will make Abraham's name great.

During times when God chooses to bless us or make our name great, remember this lesson: He blesses us *so that* we will be a blessing. What do you tend to do with your blessings and good name? Hold them tight for yourself? Use them for yourself? Or do you find ways to use them to be a blessing and honor God?

Everlasting Covenant Promise 3: I Will Bless Those Who Bless You, and Him Who Dishonors You I Will Curse

The land God showed to Abraham and promised to give his descendants was the land of Canaan—"the promised land." That land is where the country of Israel is today (and more). One day Israel will be the place where Jesus reigns on earth during the millennium after His second coming (but with the complete borders outlined in Genesis 15:18–21). Therefore we are wise to bless both the physical nation of Israel as well as the spiritual nation of Israel (Christians) because God has said to Abraham and his descendants that those who bless them will be blessed and those who curse them will be cursed. He repeats this promise throughout Scripture.

If for no other reason, we should bless Jews and the Jewish state of Israel out of honor for Jesus. Jesus descended from Abraham, Isaac, and Jacob. He was born to a Jewish virgin named Mary. God came down from heaven to take on the sins of the world, and the womb He chose to enter the world through was Mary's. This should be reason enough to honor the Jews, even today. Our Messiah was one of them.

Everlasting Covenant Promise 4: In You (Your Offspring) All the Families of the Earth Shall Be Blessed

Later in Genesis God expounded upon this promise to Abraham to specify that all the families of the earth shall be blessed through Abraham's offspring. He confirmed this promise with Isaac and also with

Jacob (whose name was changed to Israel). As we've seen, it is through *this* line that Jesus, the Messiah, came (see Matt. 1). Jesus would be the One who would make Abraham's descendants "as numerous as the stars." Jesus made Abraham not only have physical descendants but spiritual descendants, so his offspring are now as numerous as the stars. And it is through the gift of salvation through Jesus that "all the families of the earth shall be blessed." In every way, God keeps His promises.

A Series of Surrenders

We can trust God to keep His promises. But even in the midst of such great promises, like most of us, Abraham wasn't able to surrender his *entire* life all at once. He simply surrendered enough for each step. His life was a series of surrenders until finally, toward the end of his life, nothing was off the table if God asked him for it—even when God tested him to see if he would give up his son. Abraham's life was totally surrendered by the end, but early on it was harder for him. What is interesting, though, is that after each successful surrender, God rewarded him by expounding more upon His promises. It was as if God was patiently waiting in silence for Abraham to obey before confiding more.

I believe God does this with us today. He waits for obedience before confiding more. If we disobey or stay stuck in our own stuff, we may miss out on hearing Him speak. When we disobey or stay stuck, it simply means we don't have a healthy fear of God in our lives. One of my favorite verses is Psalm 25:14, which says, "The friendship of the Lord is for those who fear him, and he makes known to them his covenant." The NIV puts it this way, "The Lord confides in those who fear him; he makes his covenant known to them." Abraham's life proved this concept because with every new surrender in obedience, God confided more of His promise to him.

Abraham immediately obeyed God's first command to leave his country, but his obedience was delayed in the second and the third commands. Abraham immediately left his country when asked but allowed his father, Terah, and nephew, Lot, to join him on the journey. This was delayed obedience to the second command of God to set himself apart from his kindred. Then Abraham allowed his father, Terah, to convince him to stay in Haran, which was delayed obedience to the third command of God to go to the land He would show them.

Scripture says Abraham did not leave Haran until his father passed away, which probably meant his obedience to God was delayed a long time because the Bible says that after Terah died, Abraham took his wife, Sarai, and nephew, Lot, "and all their possessions that they had gathered, and all the people that they had acquired in Haran, and they set out to go to the land of Canaan" (Gen. 12:5). It takes a while to acquire a people group and possessions in a place. So Abraham's journey of surrender to the three commands was truly a process.

We see from Abraham's life that although God was patient throughout the surrender process, Abraham's lack of surrender often brought a degree of silence from God while He waited for Abraham's total surrender. But as each new step occurred, a new wave of revelation or assurance from God came.

Search your heart today. Ask God if there's any area that you haven't surrendered to Him. I have prayed for you to have the ability to surrender whatever your white knuckles might be clenching to, as mine have done so many times. I believe that when you do surrender what He's asking, you will hear Him speak.

CHAPTER 7

Two Types of Believers (Abraham & Lot)

WE'VE ALL HAD THEM—FRIENDS who say they're Christians, but you really can't tell. Jesus said you would know a tree by its fruit. With a little over 70 percent of the population in the United States who claim to be Christians,[27] it seems there are either a lot of people out there with a false sense of eternal security or there are a lot of spiritually sick "trees." I'm sure you've personally known someone like this. Their salvation experience seems authentic, but it's just hard to see the difference between the world and them. A typological picture of a believer who is growing into a faith-filled walk can be seen in the life of Abraham. In contrast we find that his nephew Lot's life is a picture of the believer who is saved but continues to walk by sight instead of ever learning to walk by faith.[28]

Even though Abraham became well known as a man of faith, his journey did not begin so faith-filled. He had to grow in faith through a process of willingness. Even when he was more seasoned and should have known better, we can find him faltering in faith from time to time, just like us.

Abraham, his wife Sarah, and his nephew Lot finally made it to Canaan—the land God promised. But, as a test of faith, a famine came upon the land. Abraham reacted as his flesh naturally led him and took matters into his own hands. He left Canaan and went down to Egypt where he logically knew there would be food instead of inquiring of God.

Egypt was a place full of idolatry, and Abraham became afraid once they arrived there. His wife Sarah was a beautiful woman, and he was afraid that if the Egyptians saw her, they would want her and would kill him in order to have her. Because of this fear, he told Sarah to lie to the people and tell them she was his sister. The Pharaoh ended up taking Sarah, which Abraham allowed because he was afraid. Since Abraham did not protect Sarah, the chosen bearer of the line of Jesus, God did. God sent plagues to Pharaoh and his house until he relinquished Sarah back to Abraham.

When Pharaoh understood Abraham had lied to him and brought trouble upon him, he kicked Abraham and Sarah out of Egypt. Even though they got kicked out, they had acquired Egyptian servants, livestock, silver, and gold while they were there, so they left rich. We shall soon see that these things they acquired would become a snare because it was outside of God's original plan.

What usually happens when we walk our own paths? We get into a tangled mess. Initially, after leaving Egypt, Abraham and Sarah might have thought their wayward venture had been a good deal for them, but they would soon find the effects would create heartache. From this wayward venture into Egypt came the acquisition of the Egyptian servant, Hagar. When Abraham's wife Sarah stopped believing God's promise that she would have a child of her own, she eventually gave Hagar to Abraham. The Egyptian maidservant Hagar and Abraham would bear Ishmael, who would become a point of stark division in the family. In addition, once Abraham and Sarah returned to Canaan with all their newly acquired livestock, the place where they were camping

TWO TYPES OF BELIEVERS (ABRAHAM & LOT)

would no longer be able to support all the animals they had acquired; therefore Lot's herdsman and Abraham's herdsman began to quarrel.

Even at this early point in his spiritual journey, Abraham knew it was in God's character to be a peacemaker, so Abraham told Lot and his herdsman to separate from him and his herdsman so the quarrels would stop and the animals could have enough food.

Abraham was already beginning to learn that surrendering to God often meant dying to our own "rights" for the sake of God's cause. So, for the sake of peace among God's people, Abraham told his nephew that he could have first choice of the piece of land he wanted. Keep in mind that the promise of land was given to Abraham and his line, not Lot. But Abraham acted generously and selflessly as he offered Lot his choice of the best in order to make peace with no hard feelings.

I need to take a little break from the narrative for a minute to expound upon this concept a little more. As believers we are called to die to ourselves. Over and over in Scripture we see this concept. We die to our flesh so we can live to Christ when He asks something like this of us. In Matthew 16:24, Jesus says, "If anyone would come after me, let him deny himself and take up his cross [instrument of death] and follow me." Notice Jesus didn't say, "Hang on your cross and then get back off of it and follow Me." He said to take up your cross for the journey and follow, as if there would be multiple deaths to self along the way. Dying to self is not a once-and-done event. We don't deny ourselves just for salvation and, after we've made a salvation decision, pick up where we left off before we got saved. Rather, it's a journey of denying ourselves for the sake of following Christ honorably. Like Abraham, most of us at the moment of salvation are unable to die to self completely. God asks of us in stages what He knows we can handle. This is called the sanctification *process*.

What really sets a Christian apart from the world? Many of the answers I hear from believers when I ask this question are characteristic answers like "being kind," "being nice," or "going out of your way to bless someone," but is that really it? Don't get me wrong. I think being a believer means we will exhibit these qualities and habits as well, but it's just that I know many nonbelievers who exhibit these particular characteristics better than a lot of Christians. If many nonbelievers can exhibit these things in their own willpower, then these are not the characteristics that show the power of Christ in a person's life. Do you know what does? A collection of characteristics in a person's life such as

- true selflessness,
- the absence of greed,
- extravagant generosity,
- outrageous forgiveness,
- self-denial for the sake of peace or reconciliation,
- extending absolutely undeserved grace,
- laying down your "life" (rights) for a friend's sake, and
- praying for your enemies and loving them rather than trying to get vengeance.

Though this list isn't complete, my point is the qualities that Christians should have that set them apart from the world are qualities that can *only* come by the consistent work of the Spirit in our lives. It takes the power of God at work in a person to exhibit these qualities consistently. Are we seeking God to a degree that allows Him to work in our lives enough to produce these things?

My husband and I have a friend named Chris. Years ago when Chris had his very first car, he worked and earned enough money to upgrade the car's stereo. He was so proud of it. But shortly after the new stereo was installed, it was stolen one night as the car sat in his driveway. The situation was only made worse when he found out the person who stole his stereo was a good friend of his. Chris was so angry and wanted vengeance. But Chris's father, who was a faith-filled Christian, told him, "No, son. We are called as Christians to pray for our enemies. Your stereo will be outdated in a matter of months, but the soul of the one who took your things is eternal. His soul is more important than your stereo." So Chris and his father got down on their knees. Chris waited for his father to start praying, but his dad said, "No, son. You were the one who was wronged. You have to be the one to pray."

Chris mustered up the heart and prayed for his friend who had stolen his stereo. As he prayed, he began to feel the weight lift from his shoulders. He was no longer as angry. Instead he found himself wanting his friend to find Jesus more than he wanted vengeance.

One day later on they heard a knock at the door. Chris answered the door and found his friend standing there with the stolen stereo in his hands. Tears were streaming down his friend's cheeks as he confessed, "I'm so sorry. I'm not sure why I did it." Chris told him he knew it was him all along but decided to pray for him instead of seeking vengeance. As they sat in Chris's living room that day, His friend invited Christ to be the Lord of his life too.

If Chris had initiated vengeance for himself, the events would have played out a lot differently. Do you know what one of the truest marks of a faith-filled person of Christ is? Grace. But in order to show grace, we often have to deny ourselves or our "rights" for the sake of the eternal, whether that means refraining from taking vengeance and praying for our enemy's soul instead or generously giving up something that is rightfully ours for the sake of reconciliation. Remember what Jesus said in Luke 6:27–32, 35–36:

> But I say to you who hear, love your enemies, do good to those who hate you, bless those who curse you, pray for those who abuse you. To the one who strikes you on the cheek, offer the other also, and from the one who takes away your cloak do not withhold your tunic either. Give to everyone who begs from you, and from one who takes

away your goods do not demand them back. As you wish that others would do to you, do so to them. If you love those who love you, what benefit is that to you? For even sinners love those who love them. . . . But love your enemies, and do good, and lend, expecting nothing in return, and your reward will be great, and you will be sons of the Most High, for He is kind to the ungrateful and evil. Be merciful, even as your Father is merciful.

For the sake of peace, Abraham held eternal things higher than temporal things and offered Lot his choice of the land. It's at this point in the narrative that we first see Lot as the picture of a believer who is saved but walks by his flesh rather than by faith. Hundreds of years later in the New Testament, 2 Peter 2:7 says "[God] rescued *righteous* Lot" (italics mine). Since Lot was ultimately declared "righteous" in the New Testament, we know he was saved. But despite his eternal salvation and ultimate standing before God, the Old Testament Scriptures indicate his soul was driven by his flesh, rather than by the Spirit, most of his life. In Genesis 13:8–13, notice the motivating factors in Lot's decision about which piece of land to choose (italics mine):

> Abram said to Lot, "Let there be no strife between you and me, and between your herdsmen and my herdsmen, for we are kinsmen. Is not the whole land before you? Separate yourself from me. If you take the left hand, then I will go to the right, or if you take the right hand, then I will go to the left." And Lot *lifted up his eyes and saw* that the Jordan Valley was well watered everywhere like the garden of the Lord, *like the land of Egypt*, in the direction of Zoar. (This was before the Lord destroyed Sodom and Gomorrah.) So Lot chose for himself all the Jordan Valley, and Lot journeyed east. Thus they separated from each other. Abram settled in the land of Canaan, while Lot settled among the cities of the valley and moved his tent as far as *Sodom*. Now *the men of Sodom were wicked, great sinners against the Lord*.

Lot based his decision on what his flesh saw rather than on faith in the promises of God. He looked for a land that "looked" like the idolatrous land of Egypt and moved his tent toward Sodom where the men were wicked and great sinners against the Lord. In other words, Lot had no interest in keeping his heart set apart and clean from the evils of the world. He was looking to mimic what Egypt had been to him (a source of wealth) and didn't care if it was corrupt. Greed made Lot overlook the evils of Sodom.

One day after Abraham and Lot had separated, a battle ensued between five kings from five cities against four kings from four cities. The king of Sodom (where Lot was living) lost the battle. So the enemy came and took all the possessions of Sodom and Gomorrah and they also took Lot. That's exactly what our unseen Enemy does when a believer dangles their foot in the world too long. He snares us and takes us captive before we can see it coming.

Thankfully word got around to Abraham that his nephew had been captured by the enemy. Abraham, a picture of the believer who walks by faith, knew he had to do what James 5:19–20 says, "My brothers, if anyone among you wanders from the truth and someone brings him back, let him know that whoever brings back a sinner from his wandering will save his soul from death and will cover a multitude of sins." So Abraham gathered his army and went in pursuit to defeat the enemy and bring back Lot and his possessions and all the women and the people who had gone with him. When we see a brother or sister in Christ entangled in sin, ensnared by the Enemy, we have a responsibility, which is set forth in Galatians 6:1–2: "Brothers, if anyone is caught in any transgression, you who are spiritual should restore him in a spirit of gentleness. Keep watch on yourselves, lest you too be tempted. Bear one another's burdens, and so fulfill the law of Christ."

Sodom and Gomorrah

We've all heard the story of Sodom and Gomorrah, right? It's almost as famous as the story of Noah and the ark. In Genesis 18, three "men" appear to Abraham. He soon discovers that the three men were actually two angels and an Old Testament appearance of the eternal Jesus. (Each Old Testament appearance of the eternal Jesus is called a "theophany.") The two angels gave Abraham a message about the child that would be born to him and Sarah and then headed toward their mission. The mission of the two angels was to destroy Sodom and Gomorrah because the outcry to God against Sodom and Gomorrah had become very great and the sin of those in the city had become very grave. The two angels departed toward Sodom, but the Lord Jesus stayed back with Abraham.

Knowing that his nephew Lot was living at the gates of Sodom, Abraham became worried and drew near to ask the Lord, "Will you indeed sweep away the righteous with the wicked? Suppose there are fifty righteous within the city. Will you then sweep away the place and not spare it for the fifty righteous who are in it?" The Lord answered, "If I find at Sodom fifty righteous in the city, I will spare the whole place for their sake." But Abraham was still worried: What if there wasn't fifty? So He asked the Lord, "What if there are only forty-five?" But the Lord said, "I will not destroy it if I find forty-five there." Abraham said, "What about forty?" The Lord said, "For the sake of forty, I will not do it." Abraham continued asking whether the Lord would destroy it for the sake of thirty and then twenty and finally ten. The Lord answered saying He would not destroy the city if He found ten righteous people there (Gen. 18:22–33, partly paraphrased for brevity).

After a series of events that proved just how corrupt Sodom was, the angels told Lot and his two daughters to get out of Sodom because they were about to destroy it in judgment. But the Scripture says that Lot lingered and so evil men of Sodom grabbed him.

Lot lingered. If two angels showed up and told you a judgment of destruction was about to come to your city and you needed to get out, would you linger? This shows how much his heart was tied to the corrupt city. When we allow corrupt things into our hearts and minds, we grow to love engaging with those things—the very things that will destroy us before we know it. But when we surrender our hearts and minds to the Word of God and the things of God, our ties to the things of the world become less and less. And in some way that I cannot fully explain, our hearts become more passionate and life-filled because of surrender to God.

Once Lot and his family were outside the city, the Lord rained down sulfur and fire from heaven, destroying the city, the valley, the people, and all that grew in the ground. The angels had warned Lot and his family not to look back, but as Sodom and Gomorrah were being destroyed, Lot's wife looked back and became a pillar of salt.

Salt has a lot to do with this story, and in more ways than one. Before refrigeration, salt was used as a preservative for meats and other foods. So when Lot's wife looked back, her heart was seeking the wrong thing to "preserve." She was trying to "preserve" within herself her old life in evil Sodom, and in doing that she was losing her taste. Jesus said, "You are the salt of the earth, but if salt has lost its taste, how shall its saltiness be restored? It is no longer good for anything except to be thrown out and trampled under people's feet" (Matt. 5:13). And so Lot's wife turned into a pillar of salt that had lost its saltiness, rock hard, good for nothing by way of preservation of pure things. She is being trampled underfoot there, even today. She sought to preserve her old life in Sodom but lost everything. Matthew 16:26 echoes this when it says, "For what will it profit a man if he gains the whole world and forfeits his soul?"

Still today the area of Israel where it is believed Sodom and Gomorrah was located is a barren, desert land, good for nothing. As an application, we all leave some sort of legacy. How's yours looking?

But there's another aspect of salt in the story of Sodom and Gomorrah. Jesus said to believers, "You are the salt of the earth." Remember how the angels couldn't destroy Sodom until they got Lot and his family out? We know Lot's soul was saved, although there was no real indication that he had ever learned to walk by faith instead of flesh. Once we confess in repentance, He forgives our sin and remembers it no more. Although Lot earned very few, if any, eternal crowns in heaven for his life, there's something remarkable we can learn from him. The Old Testament is detailed in its presentation of his wrong-doing, yet by the time the New Testament was written, his sin was remembered no more by the Spirit-inspired writers. Why? The eternal blood of Jesus had been shed. Jesus came as the ultimate sacrifice for sin for those in the New Testament and beyond who would believe and trust in Him, but His eternal blood also reached back to cover those of the Old Testament who had a faith that looked forward to His salvation and sacrifice. Therefore even as little faith as Lot had in his future Savior, it was enough for salvation. By the time the New Testament was divinely written, he was declared "righteous," and his sin was remembered no more.

In the New Testament, Peter, inspired by the Spirit, referred to Lot by calling him "righteous Lot," even though Genesis showed us that he liked to dangle his feet in the world (2 Pet. 2:7). Though the New Testament openly speaks of the wicked standing of unbelievers, notice how the New Testament speaks of specific believers from the Old Testament—only the good things they did by faith were remembered, even when failures had been present as well. Their faith moments are commended in celebration as if the failures had never occurred.[29] How great is our God who stands by His promise that "there is now, therefore, no condemnation for those who are in Christ Jesus our Lord" (Rom. 8:1). If you have confessed your sin with godly sorrow and have faith in the blood of Jesus, God removes your sin from His mind as far as the east is from the west. Therefore you can let the weight lift off your shoulders. You are not condemned. The blood of Jesus has covered it in full. It is remembered no more.

Lot, though wayward, was still considered salt. The salt of salvation was a preserving factor for his own soul, but it also acted as a temporary preserving factor for the city of Sodom in this story. The angels could not destroy the city until they had rescued Lot and his family out of it. Once the preserving salt of those chosen for salvation were removed, the judgment of destruction could come. "For God has not destined us for wrath, but to obtain salvation through our Lord Jesus Christ" (1 Thess. 5:9). Listen to the words of Peter recounting how God's salty ones are protected:

> If He did not spare the ancient world, but preserved Noah, a herald of righteousness, with seven others, when he brought a flood upon the world of the ungodly; if by turning the cities of Sodom and Gomorrah to ashes he condemned them to extinction, making them an example of what is going to happen to the ungodly; and if he rescued righteous Lot, greatly distressed by the sensual conduct of the wicked (for as that righteous man lived among them day after day, he was tormenting his righteous soul over their lawless deeds that he saw and heard); then the Lord knows how to rescue the godly from trials, and to keep the unrighteous under punishment until the day of judgment, and especially those who indulge in the lust of defiling passion and despise authority. (2 Pet. 2:4–10)

In the Old Testament we find literal, historical stories that help us picture what is true for us spiritually. Like the flood of Noah's time, the story of Sodom and Gomorrah is a picture of the final judgment that will come upon the earth. Until then believers are the preserving factor (salt of the earth), holding back judgment, just like in the cases of Noah and Lot. Noah was holding back judgment while building the ark before the first judgment of the flood upon the land. Lot was holding back judgment while still living in the city of Sodom. But once believers are raptured or caught up with the Lord in the air, the judgment waves of the tribulation will begin. And once the tribulation begins, the Jewish remnant and others who are to be saved after missing the rapture will be sealed by Jesus until His second coming to earth. At Jesus's second coming, the final and ultimate judgment will come to the enemies of God.

Jesus references the days of Noah and the days of Lot being "like" the judgment in the end times. Luke 17:26–37 states:

> "Just as it was in the days of Noah, so will it be in the days of the Son of Man. They were eating and drinking and marrying and being given in marriage, until the day when Noah entered the ark, and the flood came and destroyed them all. Likewise, just as it was in the days of Lot—they were eating and drinking, buying and selling, planting and building, but on the day when Lot went out from Sodom, fire and sulphur rained from heaven and destroyed them all—so it will be in the day when the Son of Man is revealed. On that day, let the one who is on the housetop, with his goods in the house, not come down to take them away, and likewise let the one who is in the field not turn back. Remember Lot's wife. Whoever seeks to preserve his life will lose it, but whoever loses his life will keep it. I tell you, in that night there will be two in one bed. One will be taken and the other left. There will be two women grinding together. One will be taken and the other left." And they said to Him, "Where Lord?" He said to them, "Where the corpse is, there the vultures will gather."

A lot of people read that section of Scripture and get confused thinking it means the rapture when it says, "there will be two in one bed. One will be taken and the other left. There will be two women grinding together. One will be taken and the other left." But given the other details in this passage, the rapture would have already occurred by the time we read this phrase.

These verses are actually talking about the judgment at the end of the tribulation period. These verses are written for the Jewish remnant of Israel saved after the rapture but during the tribulation. They will have our Bibles and books and all that we left behind when we were raptured. So let this truth be encouragement to them. One will be left (preserved/rescued) while the other is taken and destroyed by judgment. The believer will be left while the unbeliever is taken, swept up in judgment. Scholars believe this is the case because in the last verse, the disciples say, "Where Lord?" And Jesus says, "Where the corpse is, there the vultures will gather" (Luke 17:37). Just as the vultures have a keen eye to detect a carcass to feed on, the divine judgment will have a keen eye to detect corruption to feed on.

Scholar Warren W. Wiersbe has much to say on this passage of Scripture:

> Luke 17:30–36 describes what will occur when Jesus Christ returns in judgment to defeat His enemies and establish His kingdom on earth (Revelation 19:11–20:6). Believers in every age of the church can take warning from these verses, but they apply in a special way to Israel at the end of the age (see Matthew 24:29–44). When Jesus comes for His church and takes it to heaven, it will happen "in a moment, in the twinkling of an eye" (1 Corinthians 15:52). Nobody taking part in the rapture of the church need worry about being on a housetop or in a field and wanting to get something out of the house! However, when the Lord returns *to earth*, His coming will first be preceded by a "sign" in heaven (Matthew 24:30–31), and some people might try to hurry home to rescue something. "Remember Lot's wife!"
>
> The verb *taken* in Luke 17:34–36 does not mean "taken to heaven" but "taken away in judgment" (Matthew 24:36–41). The person "left" is a believer who enters into the Kingdom. Noah and his family

were "left" to enjoy a new beginning, while the whole population of the earth was "taken" in the flood. In spite of their sins, Lot and his daughters were "left" while the people in Sodom and Gomorrah were "taken" when the fire and brimstone destroyed the cities.

The fact that it is night in Luke 17:34 but day in Luke 17:35–36 indicates that the whole world will be involved in the return of Jesus Christ in glory. "Behold, he cometh with clouds; and every eye shall see him" (Revelation 1:7).

Three times the disciples had heard Jesus talk about people being "taken" and "left," so they asked Him a most logical question: "Where, Lord?" Our Lord's reply has the sound of a familiar proverb: "Just as the eagles [and vultures, Matt. 24:28] gather at a corpse, so the lost will be gathered together for judgment." The description of the last battle in Revelation 19:17–21 certainly parallels the image of carrion-eating birds gorging themselves on flesh.

In other words, when the Lord returns to judge His enemies, there will be a separation of the saved and the lost. Whether it be day or night, whether people are working or sleeping, the separation and judgment will come. Those who are saved will be left to enter the glorious Kingdom, while those who are lost will be taken away in judgment.

Even though the primary interpretation for these verses is for Israel in the End Times, they do emphasize for the church the importance of being ready when Jesus returns. We must not be like Lot's wife, whose heart was so in Sodom that she looked back in spite of the angels' warning (Genesis 19:17, 26). There are many professed Christians today whose plans would be interrupted if Jesus returned (note 1 Thessalonians 5:1–11)! Our Lord's warning in Luke 17:33 finds parallels in Matthew 10:39; Luke 9:24; and John 12:25, and is a fundamental principle of the Christian's life. The only way to save your life is to lose it for the sake of Christ and the gospel.

Jesus pictured civilization as a "rotting corpse" that would one day be ripe for judgment. The discerning believer sees evidence of this on every hand and realizes that the "days of Noah" and the "days of Lot" are soon on us. Our Lord can return for His church at any time, so we are not looking for signs, but we do know that the "coming events can cast their shadows before." As we see many of these things begin to come to pass (Luke 21:28), we know that His return is nearing.[30]

After Sodom and Gomorrah were destroyed, we find Lot (our picture of the believer who walks by flesh) at a place of loss. He began the journey choosing land by fleshly sight and greed, choosing the way that most looked like it would lead to wealth and prosperity. He was led by his eyes of flesh rather than led by spiritual eyes focused on the eternal. And in the end, we see that he lost his wife, his sons-in-law who didn't heed his warnings to get out, his possessions, and his wealth. He barely escaped with his two daughters, and later in Scripture we find that he lived the rest of his life in a cave. Lot is a real-life testimony to 1 Corinthians 3:12–15:

> Now if anyone builds on the foundation with gold, silver, precious stones, wood, hay, straw—each one's work will become manifest, for the Day [of Judgment] will disclose it, because it will be revealed by fire, and the fire will test what sort of work each one has done. If the work that anyone has built on the foundation survives, he will receive a reward. If anyone's work is burned up, he will suffer loss, though he himself will be saved, but only as through fire.

Lot was saved, but only as through fire. Most of everything else was burned up, proving his life was mostly about second things, carnal things, things that won't last—instead of being about first things, eternal things, things that last and reflect the beauty of the One who saved him.

What are you building with on your foundation of salvation? Are you building with temporal pursuits like wood, hay, or straw that will burn up in the fire? Or are you building with eternal pursuits like gold, silver, and precious stones that only become more refined and more beautiful with fire?

Jude 1:17–23

But you must remember, beloved, the predictions of the apostles of our Lord Jesus Christ. They said to you, "In the last time there will be scoffers, following their own ungodly passions." It is these who cause divisions, worldly people, devoid of the Spirit. But you, beloved, building yourself up in your most holy faith and praying in the Holy Spirit, keep yourselves in the love of God, waiting for the mercy of our Lord Jesus Christ that leads to eternal life. And have mercy on those who doubt; save others by snatching them out of the fire; to others show mercy with fear, hating even the garment stained by the flesh.

CHAPTER 8

The Waging War
(Isaac vs. Ishmael; Jacob vs. Esau)

WHEN WE STUDY HISTORY or even listen to the evening news, we can always find a war going on between good and evil. The war is literal, but it is also spiritual. I believe it is possible that wars between good and evil in the physical actually begin in the spiritual and end up bleeding into the physical. There is always a war waging around us in the heavenlies. Ephesians 6:12 says, "For we do not wrestle against flesh and blood, but against the rulers, against the authorities, against the cosmic powers over this present darkness, against the spiritual forces of evil in the heavenly places."

The division that happened between Isaac and Ishmael and later between Jacob and Esau was no different. We are going to first look at the split between Isaac and Ishmael and the rippling effect that shows even today.

Isaac vs. Ishmael

Most of us know how the story began. God promised Abraham that he and Sarah would have a son, even though Sarah was barren. It was through that son that God's promises would be passed. All Abraham had to do was wait for God to fulfill His promise in His own good time. But Abraham and Sarah began to grow restless waiting on God. They began to worry that they were growing too old to bear children.

Therefore, when Sarah offered her Egyptian maidservant to Abraham to bear a child for their family, Abraham jumped on the opportunity without consulting God. This decision played right into the plans of the spiritual forces of evil who were plotting defeat and destruction for God's people. After Abraham slept with Sarah's Egyptian maidservant, Hagar, Hagar bore a son and named him Ishmael. Well, I'll tell you right now, two mommas fighting over a boy they both believe to be rightfully "theirs" never goes well. The situation was immediately off to a rocky start.

Fast-forward thirteen years. If Sarah considered herself too old to have children when she gave Hagar to Abraham thirteen years ago, by this point she is *really* too old to have children. In fact the Scriptures describe her womb to have been "as good as dead." But God promised what He had promised, and His timing is impeccable. Unbeknownst to them God was waiting to bring life from a dead womb. That's just like God, isn't it? Life from death, as if to be a picture of Christ's resurrection from the dead and a picture of our life dead to sin but made alive to God in Christ Jesus.

Eventually, by a miracle of God, Sarah had a son in her old age and named him Isaac. But now there was a new problem. God's plan and promise rested with the son He had promised all along, the legitimate son, Isaac, not Ishmael. Ishmael had been a desperate attempt by Sarah to fill a deep longing and desire for a child too soon. Now that she had her own, the hard feelings between Sarah and Hagar intensified. Rage. Anger. Jealousy. Hate. Competition. Hagar and Sarah despised each other; Isaac and Ishmael had drama. Enmity between the two families was born. Sarah became so angry with the other woman and her son that she told Abraham to send Hagar and Ishmael away. Abraham was troubled, torn between his two sons—one legitimate, the other illegitimate—yet he loved both.

God spoke to Abraham and told him to send Hagar and Ishmael away like Sarah had asked, but in order to comfort Abraham, God assured him that He would also make a great nation of Ishmael. Genesis 17:20–21 says, "As for Ishmael, I have heard you; behold, I have blessed him and will make him fruitful and multiply him greatly. He shall father twelve princes, and I will make him into a great nation. But I will establish my covenant with Isaac." Time would prove God's words to be true. God's covenant was established with Isaac's line, and this line ran through God's Jewish people, Israel. Through this line also came Jesus, the promised Messiah. But God's Word held true for Ishmael's line as well. Ishmael's line became a numerous people who were perpetual enemies of Israel throughout the Old Testament, known as the Ishmaelites. Today Ishmael's line is believed to be traced to the Arab people, Muslims, and Muhammad, the prophet and founder of Islam. In the book, *Encountering the World of Islam*, it is noted:

> The tribes of Muhammad's Arabia, and Muslims to this day, trace their heritage back to Ishmael, Abraham's son by Hagar, not to Isaac, Abraham's son by Sarah. Unfortunate circumstances led Hagar to flee her home, but God had great compassion for her. When Ishmael was born, God promised Hagar that her descendants would be too numerous to count (Gen. 16:9–11; 17:20; 21:8–21; 25:13–16). Today more than 1.6 billion Muslims (one of every five people) identify with her.[31]

History shows there has been perpetual conflict both between Muslims and Jews and Muslims and Christians. The promise given by the angel of the Lord to Hagar while she was pregnant with Ishmael further reveals that Ishmael's line and Isaac's line would be against each other:

I will surely multiply your offspring so that they cannot be numbered for multitude. Behold, you are pregnant and shall bear a son. You shall call him Ishmael, because the Lord has listened to your affliction. He shall be a wild donkey of a man, his hand shall be against everyone and everyone's hand against him, and he shall dwell over against all his kinsmen. (Gen. 16:10–12)

And that is exactly what has happened between the two lines for centuries. This severance between the two mothers and their sons is the origin of the divisions between the followers of Judaism and Christianity and the followers of Islam. Christianity and Islam are the two largest religions today—one drawing its heritage from the line of Isaac, and the other drawing its heritage from the line of Ishmael.

Personally, though, as a side note, I have such a heart for Muslims. I want them to know the truth about Jesus so they can live eternally with us and have peace. I want them to see that their Quran actually encourages them to read the Bible, and it supports, at least, that Jesus was the most supernatural prophet that ever lived. The miraculous way Jesus is described in the Quran has got to mean something. Many don't even know what's in the Quran or the Bible to be able to make a choice between them. They've been content to stay blinded.

Since the events of 9/11, among Americans there seems to be a sort of blanket stigma against Muslims. What we often forget is that it was radical Islamic extremists who performed the terrorist attacks of September 11, 2001. A friend and I recently visited an Islamic mosque as extra credit for a seminary class. The women there were hospitable, welcoming, and kind to us. They brought us water bottles and sincerely wanted to make us feel welcome, even after they found out we were Christians. Sure, our religions differ on the important points, but the people of that religion aren't so different from you and me inside. I think it's important to love them and remember them in our prayers. There's nothing that drives a person to pray more passionately than genuine love.

The Religion of Islam

Muhammad, the prophet and founder of Islam, had a difficult childhood. He was an orphan by age six. After the death of his mother, he was entrusted to his grandfather, but his grandfather did not live long and so he was eventually entrusted to his uncle.[32] Although Muhammad grew to be noticeably gifted with people, Muslims generally believe he was illiterate.[33] Despite being unable to read, he seemed to be a devout worshiper of Allah. Allah simply means "God," and Muhammad was intent that Allah was the only God to be worshiped. Many have wondered whether Muhammad learned about Allah or God through tradition, as it was passed down through the generations from Abraham, or whether random Jews and Christians that Muhammad encountered told him about God.[34] Regardless, it must be noted that it is highly debated whether the name Allah is referring to the same God as the One of the Old Testament or not. But I will add as a sidenote that the Allah described in the Quran is very different than the God described in the Bible in many ways like how Allah never enters into his creation, offers no real redemption and remedy for sin, offers no assurance of salvation, and how he views humanity as slaves rather than sons and daughters. These are just a few of the differences. Whole books could be written on this subject.

According to tradition, at the age of forty Muhammad received his first revelation from the angel Gabriel. The angel came to him and told him to "Recite in the name of your Lord who created, created man from clots of blood" (Sura 96:1–2). Understandably the angel told him to recite rather than write, since he was illiterate. Two years later he began to have more revelations from the angel Gabriel. After Muhammad died his followers wrote down the messages he had recited and bound them into a book called the Quran which means "recitation."[35]

The Quran tells several stories from the Old Testament and New Testament but with large discrepancies and contradictions, many of which cannot be reconciled. Muhammad, who lived a good number of generations after Jesus, had likely encountered Christians or Jews who told him stories from the Bible. But even if Muhammad had been literate, he probably had no way of reading the Bible. The book *Encountering the World of Islam* notes, "At the time Islam began, Arabia lacked a biblical witness: Muhammad and the Arab peoples had no Bible in their language. . . . The Bible was not translated into Arabic until AD 837 and not published (beyond a few scholarly manuscripts) until 1516."[36] Since Muhammad died in 632, the Bible translations were too late. Ironically he affirmed the Scriptures to be true, even though the Quran contradicts the Bible at many points and denies Jesus as the Son of God.

What's concerning is that the validity of the Quran is based entirely on a visitation from an angel. No further proof or witness is given to the words of the Quran. The New Testament (which was written long before the Quran) has a warning about this. Galatians 1:8 says, "But even if we or an angel from heaven should preach to you a gospel contrary to the one we preached to you, let him be accursed." The "gospel" contained in the Quran is most certainly contrary to the one both Jesus and the eye witnesses of Jesus's miracles and resurrection had proclaimed. As such, this new "gospel" was brought to Muhammed by an angel, just as Galatians warns.

Galatians 1:8 allows us to realize that there are good angels, but there are also bad angels who want to deceive people and confuse the true gospel of Christ. I believe in the possibility of angel visitation, but the angel's words should align with Scripture if they are to be trusted.

Additionally, the Quran tells different versions of the stories and words of Jesus. So which version is correct? The writers of the Quran were not living at the time of Jesus. They didn't live until about six centuries later. The writers of the New Testament were living at the time of Jesus. The bigger the span between the event and the writing about that event, the less reputable that writing becomes from a scholarly standpoint.

Muhammad affirmed the Scriptures to be true. So when Muslims later began to realize there were great discrepancies between Muhammad's recitations in the Quran and the Bible, they decided the Scriptures were true in their original form but were translated into other languages incorrectly. This is how contradictions between the Bible and the Quran are often explained by Muslims. The book *Encountering the World of Islam* says the problem with this stance in Islam is "manuscripts of both the Old and New Testaments, dating back to several hundred years before Muhammad, were placed in museums and are intact today."[37] If Muhammad affirmed the Scriptures during his time, but later Muslims claim they have been changed, all one has to do is go back to see that the translations of the Bible we have today can be verified with the earliest manuscripts dated before the time of Muhammad, and they do. Additionally, we have the Dead Sea Scrolls that were discovered that confirm the Bible we have today.

In her autobiography, *I Dared to Call Him Father*, Bilquis Sheikh, a former Muslim, tells about her journey to faith in Christ. After she became a Christian, she began witnessing to other Muslims as opportunities presented themselves. This particular conversation from her book is helpful in understanding the Muslim misconception about the Bible:

> "Begum," the man said, "one thing really disturbs me about Muslims who convert to Christianity. It is the Bible. We all know that the Christian New Testament has been changed from what God gave."
>
> He was expressing Islam's main charge against the Bible, that it had been so altered that today's version is untrustworthy. The original, Muslims claim, had agreed with the Quran.
>
> "I hope you won't think I'm being facetious," I said. "I really do want to know something. I've heard often that the Bible was changed but I've never been able to learn who changed it. When were the changes made and what passages were corrupted?"

My visitor leaned back and looked up at the ceiling, his fingers drumming the arm of his chair. He did not answer. It was unfair of me, I guess. As far as I knew there were no answers to these questions.

"You see," I went on, drawing on research I had made, "in the British Museum there are ancient versions of the Bible which were published nearly three hundred years before Muhammad was born. On every issue between Christianity and Islam these old manuscripts are identical with today's Bible. The experts say that in every basic essential today's Bible had not been changed from the original. This is important for me personally. For to me the Bible has become an alive Word. It speaks to my soul and feeds me. It helps guide me. . ."

My visitor got to his feet in the middle of my sentence.

". . . and so," I went on, "I find it quite important to know if there really are places where I'm fooling myself. Can you tell me?"

"You talk about the 'Word' almost as if it were living," my visitor said.

"I believe Christ is living, if that's what you mean," I said. "The Quran itself says that Christ was the Word of God. I would love to talk to you about it sometime."

"I must be going."

And that was that.[38]

Excerpt from I Dared to Call Him Father, *by Bilquis Sheikh and Richard H. Schneider, copyright © 1978, 2003. Used by permission of Chosen Books, a division of Baker Publishing Group.*

I went to dinner with a Muslim woman a few years ago. I didn't know much about the Muslim religion at the time, so I was excited to talk with her. We had a nice dinner discussing family, life plans, and dreams, but after dinner I asked, "I've got to know. Do you believe in Jesus?" I was expecting her to say no, and then I was planning on sharing the gospel with her in a non-threatening, caring way, as I didn't want to make her feel like I was forcing Christianity on her. I just felt like it would be wrong if I had such a life-changing gospel and didn't at least offer it to her. But when she heard my question, her face lit up and she said, "Yes! I believe in Jesus! We call Him Isa!" I was so confused. I said, "Wait—you do? Like . . . do you believe that He was the Messiah?" And she said, "Yes!"

So I left that evening thinking, "Okay, so she calls herself a Muslim but she's secretly a Christian?" But after studying Islam a little more, I realized that I didn't ask the right question. Muslims believe that Jesus is one of their great prophets. They believe He came and performed great miracles. They even believe Jesus is the Messiah. Christians understand Messiah to mean "the promised Savior," but the literal translation simply means "anointed one." So Muslims say He was "anointed" by God because He was able to do miracles, and therefore they accept the title Messiah for that reason alone. However they do not believe Jesus is divine or the Son of God. They simply believe He was a good man and a prophet who God equipped to do great miracles.

If I had asked my friend that night, "Do you believe Jesus is the Son of God?" our conversation would have gone very differently. Muslims do not believe in Jesus's divinity or Sonship to God. They are adamant that there is only *one* God, so the idea of the Trinity in Christianity seems like the worship of multiple gods to them.

It is often falsely believed that Muslims worship Muhammad. This, however, is not accurate either. They only believe Muhammad to be a prophet like Moses or Noah or any of the other prophets of God in history. To worship more than one God would be idolatry, and they are steadfastly against that. That's why the Trinity of Christianity feels like idolatry to them. The concept of the Trinity is one of the main points that keeps a Muslim from considering Christianity.

Bilquis Sheikh does a good job clarifying to a Muslim what the Trinity of Christianity truly means:

> You perhaps have heard of Sadhu Sundar Singh, the devout Sikh to whom Jesus appeared in a vision. This is how Jesus explained

the Trinity to him: "Just as in the sun there are both heat and light, but the light is not heat and the heat is not light, but both are one, though in their manifestation they have different forms, so I and the Holy Spirit, proceeding from the Father, bring light and heat to the world... Yet We are not three but One, just as the sun is but one."[39]

Excerpt from I Dared to Call Him Father *by Bilquis Sheikh and Richard H. Schneider, copyright © 1978, 2003. Used by permission of Chosen Books, a division of Baker Publishing Group*

Muslims reject Jesus as the Son of God because of confusion over the Trinity. This is a detrimental mistake. Before Muhammad was born, and before Islam was even an official religion, the apostle John of the New Testament wrote a special warning concerning antichrists that would come. The warning emphasized that no one who denies the Son has God, the Father:

> I write to you, not because you do not know the truth, but because you know it, and because no lie is of the truth. Who is the liar but he who denies that Jesus is the Christ? This is the Antichrist, he who denies the Father and the Son. No one who denies the Son has the Father. Whoever confesses the Son has the Father also. Let what you heard from the beginning abide in you. If what you heard from the beginning abides in you, then you too will abide in the Son and in the Father. And this is the promise that he made to us—eternal life. I write these things to you about those who are trying to deceive you. (1 John 2:21–26)

And there are many other verses in Scripture that speak to the fact that the only way to the Father is through the Son. Jesus Himself says,

> In my Father's house are many rooms. If it were not so, would I have told you that I go to prepare a place for you? And if I go and prepare

a place for you, I will come again and will take you to myself, that where I am you may be also. . . . I am the way, and the truth, and the life. No one comes to the Father except through me. If you had known me, you would have known my Father also. From now on you do know him and have seen him. (John 14:2, 6–7)

Jesus claims divinity and Sonship.

As you can see, there are a lot of holes in Islam and a lot of confusion toward Christianity within the religion of Islam. All it takes is someone caring enough to learn a little about their faith in order to be able to sit down and have conversations with our Muslim neighbors. From my experience, they are surprisingly open to talking about their faith and hearing about ours. The book *Encountering the World of Islam* is a great starting place and has been referenced several times in the writing of this chapter. The book points out that "few Christians have reached out to Muslims. Even today, although 37 percent of all non-Christians are Muslims, perhaps 10 percent of missionaries work among them."[40]

When I think of Muslims, I think of Christ's words in Luke 10:2, "The harvest is plentiful, but the laborers are few. Therefore pray earnestly to the Lord of the harvest to send out laborers into his harvest." The book *Encountering the World of Islam* confirms this reality: "More Muslims have come to Christ in the last forty years than in the previous 1350 years combined."[41] As we get closer and closer to the culmination of the end times, God is beginning to miraculously stir in both Muslims and Jews. He's giving Muslims dreams and visions and they are coming to salvation *despite* the fact that they have a very good chance of being killed or cast out from their family for walking away from Islam and turning to Christianity. To accept Jesus they truly have to be willing to die for their faith. But Jesus calls us to forsake all in order to follow Him because He is the only way to eternal salvation.

The Muslims who have come to salvation in Christ have taken the risk because they understand that it is better to die early in this life and have eternal life than to try to save our lives in this world and lose our eternity with Christ. As Christians we are called to take the gospel to the ends of the earth, and I believe that includes Muslims and Jews, whom we have for so long forsaken. Let's go and share the true gospel with them before it's too late. The harvest is plentiful.

The Cave of Machpelah

Islam is the newest of the three religions claiming Abraham as patriarch. The prophet Muhammad declared his heritage through the line of Ishmael. Judaism and Christianity claim their heritage through the line of Isaac. We continue to see the effects of this division between Muslims, Christians, and Jews. The source of one of the points of disagreement today has its start in Genesis 23. When Sarah died, Abraham bought a piece of land in Hebron (modern-day Israel) that had a cave to use as a burial place. This cave was called the Cave of Machpelah. Abraham buried Sarah there, and later Isaac and Ishmael reunited to bury their father, Abraham, in the same cave.

The cave is therefore important to all three of the Abrahamic religions. The Jews built a structure over it as a place for prayers and gatherings to honor the patriarchs. Then eventually an ancient Christian church was built over the cave as a monument. Then the Muslims conquered Hebron and made it a Muhammadian mosque and refused entry to the Jews. Though the violence over this holy site has lessened now, Jews struggle to regain prayer rights there even today. All of this turmoil exists because Abraham is buried there and is the patriarch of all three religions.[42]

There are additional patriarchs buried in this cave that I have yet to mention. Burial caves, such as this one, were used to bury generations of family members. When we follow the generations buried in this cave, it is through the line of Isaac (the bloodline of the Israelites of the Old Testament and eventually Jesus)—and not the line of Ishmael (the bloodline of the Arabs and Muhammad). Scripture identifies six people who were buried here. It is as if the six buried in this cave (also known as "the cave of the patriarchs") were divinely orchestrated in order to confirm the chosen line of validity. Here are the individuals buried in the cave: Abraham and his wife Sarah; Isaac and his wife, Rebekah; and Jacob and his wife Leah. The ones buried in the cave of the patriarchs follow the line of Abraham, Isaac, and Jacob. Isaac is included while Ishmael is left out.

Second of all, and perhaps more intriguing, some of these men had other wives during their lifetime, but only certain wives were buried with them in this cave. Abraham chose another wife after Sarah died, but his second wife wasn't buried there; Jacob loved Rachel, and chose her as his wife but was tricked by his soon-to-be father-in-law into marrying Leah first. Although Jacob loved Rachel more and eventually married her too, Leah was the line through which Jesus would be born. Therefore the Cave of the Patriarchs not only follows the line of Abraham, Isaac, and Jacob but also follows the specific wives through which Jesus, the promised Messiah, would come. God, in His sovereignty, orchestrated each specific husband-wife pair to be buried in the Cave of the Patriarchs as just one more detail to further prove the validity of Jesus while confirming the chosen line was with Isaac, not Ishmael.

Jacob and Esau

The enmity that Isaac had with his brother Ishmael seems to have been passed somehow in the womb to his two sons. Our bondages often last generations, don't they? Isaac and Rebekah were about to have twin boys. While still in her womb, the boys struggled with each other within her. So Rebekah inquired of the Lord about the struggle she felt inside her. The Lord answered, "Two nations are in your womb, and two peoples from within you shall be divided; the one shall be stronger than the other, the older shall serve the younger." Esau came out first, and Jacob came out right after holding Esau's heel. The first thing we learn of the two boys is that Esau was a skilled hunter and man of the field, and

Jacob was a quiet man who dwelled in tents (Gen. 25:27). Nimrod was also described as a great hunter. Like Nimrod, Esau would live for his flesh, make bad decisions, and become enemies with the people of God.

Isaac's favorite son was Esau because Esau would hunt game and bring home the best food. But Rebekah's favorite son was Jacob. No doubt Rebekah kept the prophesy from the Lord about her two sons close to her heart. She knew that Esau would end up serving Jacob because the Lord had told her "the older will serve the younger," and she knew somehow the birthright would have to be switched. She just didn't know how. Instead of waiting on the Lord, she plotted.

One day Esau came in from the field exhausted and hungry. Jacob had been making red stew and it smelled delicious. Esau begged Jacob for some, but Jacob and Rebekah had been plotting. So Jacob told Esau to sell him his birthright and he could have some stew. Sounds absurd, doesn't it? But here's the thing about living by your flesh: you'll take instant gratification over waiting any day, and instant gratification decisions will become a curse to you. Esau agreed to Jacob's proposal. Once he got his fill, he immediately regretted selling his birthright. He regretted it so much, he began to despise it.

As if in defiance, Esau ended up marrying from the forbidden daughters of Ishmael, causing Isaac and Rebekah much grief. But even through the grief, Esau remained Isaac's favorite and Jacob remained Rebekah's favorite. When Isaac came to the last moments of his life on his deathbed, he readied himself to issue his final blessings on his children. Isaac called Esau to him and told him to go hunt and prepare his favorite meal before he gave the blessing. I guess Isaac knew he needed to be buttered up a little before speaking a blessing over his favorite yet disobedient son who had married the Ishmaelite.

In those days within the culture of the people of God, the father, near the time of his death, would speak something over each of his children and his words would come true. It was therefore a very important moment. Esau left to go hunt. While he was gone, Rebekah and Jacob devised a plan to trick poor, blind Isaac into believing Jacob was Esau so he would give *Jacob* the blessing of the firstborn instead of Esau. The plan worked. When Esau returned and found out, he was furious!

Esau's anger burned within him toward Jacob. Rebekah overheard Esau one day, plotting to kill Jacob, so she sent Jacob off to live with her relatives until it was safe.

That's how the strife between Jacob and Esau began. But did they ever become two nations as the Lord had prophesied while they were still in Rebekah's womb? Yes! Esau's family became the nation of Edom, and Jacob's became the nation of Israel.

Throughout Scripture the nation of Edom and Israel were perpetual enemies. The Edomites assaulted Jerusalem, were involved in Nebuchadnezzar's destruction of Jerusalem (Ps. 137; Lam. 4:21), and came against many of Israel's kings throughout history. In fact the dissension continued even into Jesus's day. Turns out even Herod the Great is from the line of Esau.[43] Remember him from the story of Jesus? When he found out that the Jewish Messiah had been born, he demanded that all the baby boys under age two be killed in order to eradicate any chances of a Jewish Messiah rising to power and taking over his throne. God, however, did not allow Jesus to be killed.

Again we see the unseen spiritual battle bleeding into physical circumstances. Of course Satan wanted to kill Jesus before Jesus could give him a huge blow to the head! And Satan had many humans unknowingly at his beck and call, ready to do his dirty work (John 8:39–47). Who are you allowing yourself to be used by?

One more thing about the Edomites. There's a tiny prophetic book in the Old Testament called Obadiah, which has only twenty-one verses. The prophet Obadiah received a vision from God about Edom (the people of Esau) and was sent to warn them of their destruction because of their treatment of Israel. The prophesy came true, and the Edomites were destroyed in AD 70 in events surrounding the destruction of the temple and were never heard from again. Obadiah's vision from God came to pass: "you shall be cut off forever" (v. 10) and "there shall be no survivor for the house of Esau" (v. 18). The Word of the Lord stands true! Believe it. Trust it.

The War Within

The war between good and evil is in the world, but it is also inside of each of us. Even after we have been "born again" in Christ, our sin nature that we inherited from Adam still wars with the new Spirit dwelling inside us at times. Galatians 5:16–18 says, "But I say, walk by the Spirit, and you will not gratify the desires of the flesh. For the desires of the flesh are against the Spirit, and the desires of the Spirit are against the flesh, for these are opposed to each other, to keep you from doing the things you want to do. But if you are led by the Spirit, you are not under the law."

Isaac encountered this struggle. He was torn between the path of his own fleshly desires and the path God was asking for. Isaac knew the prophesy from the Lord about their twins. He knew God had declared that the blessing would be on Jacob, and he should have walked in obedience to that. But his flesh favored Esau for the food he brought home from great hunts. So when it came time for Isaac to bless his two sons, he stifled the knowledge that he should give the bigger blessing to Jacob and tried to give it to Esau. When he realized he had actually given the blessing to Jacob by accident just as God had said, the Scripture says, "Then Isaac trembled violently" (Gen. 27:33). I believe this was the moment of Isaac's repentance. He didn't get mad but acted out of repentance from then on.

We have all gotten tangled up in sin from time to time. We justify what we need to justify in order to satisfy what we want. We think we know better than Scripture at times. We think we know better than good, godly advice at times. We think we don't have to pray about it because we are secretly afraid the answer will be contrary to what we want. We avoid Scriptures about the subject matter or allow ourselves to twist it to make it say what we want. We walk a road we know isn't exactly right, but we walk the fence pretty well and think we can manage. Until . . .

Until, the Lord, in His infinite grace, lifts the curtain on our self-cultivated darkness and floods the situation with the truth of His light. The lightbulb comes on, and we wake up startled and think, *What have I been doing?* And we fall on our face before God *trembling* and weeping in repentance. As time passes after this sort of realization, there are moments when we look back and *tremble* at how close we were to destruction. We *tremble* at how close we were to being hardened to God. We *tremble* at the thought of everything we could have lost and how our path in life could have changed drastically. We *tremble*, just like Isaac.

We know this was Isaac's moment of true repentance, because when Esau begged for a blessing, too, Isaac refused to compromise the Word of the Lord for the first time. He was repentant and steadfast, unwilling to compromise the Word of the Lord for something as temporal as food. Instead of a blessing, Isaac gave Esau the truth that the blessing was with Jacob. Here are his words to Esau, which all came true: "Behold, away from the fatness of the earth shall your dwelling be, and away from the dew of heaven on high. By your sword you shall live, and you shall serve your brother; but when you grow restless you shall break his yoke from your neck" (Gen. 27:39–40).

There's a lesson for us in this. Isaac let Esau, who is a picture of the flesh, feed him food day by day, little by little. Isaac came to *crave* the food of the flesh until finally he wasn't led by the Spirit of the Lord much at all. He made decisions based on what his flesh wanted rather than what God had declared. I heard an illustration from Billy Graham a long time ago about the war between our flesh and spirit that has stuck with me.

> An Eskimo fisherman came to town every Saturday afternoon. He always brought his two dogs with him. One was white and the

other was black. He had taught them to fight on command. Every Saturday afternoon in the town square the people would gather and these two dogs would fight and the fisherman would take bets. On one Saturday the black dog would win; another Saturday, the white dog would win—but the fisherman always won! His friends began to ask him how he did it. He said, "I starve one and feed the other. The one I feed always wins because he is stronger."[44]

Taken from The Holy Spirit: Activating God's Power in Your Life *by Billy Graham. Copyright © 2000 by Thomas Nelson. Used by permission of Thomas Nelson. www.thomasnelson.com*

Which will we feed more, the Spirit or the flesh? Whichever one gets fed the most will win.

CHAPTER 9

Great Lengths
(Jacob)

WE HAVE A FAMILY friend who grew up hating the name given to her at birth. She hated her name so much that when she reached adulthood, she had it legally changed. Even though her name has been changed for many years now, it still fascinates me just as much as when I first heard it. I find myself pondering about what name I would choose for myself if I were to change my name. I can never decide. My name is very much part of who I am. Other names just seem foreign to me when I practice writing them as my own just to see what they would feel like. But throughout Scripture we see God often giving people new names. Abram becomes Abraham; Sarai becomes Sarah; Jacob becomes Israel. And the prophetic words of Revelation 2:17 (NASB) say, "To him who overcomes, to him I will give some of the hidden manna, and I will give him a white stone, and a new name written on the stone which no one knows but he who receives it." The concept of name changes even applies to those of us who persevere to the end.

To better understand let's look at why Jacob's name was changed in Genesis 32:22–32. The title of the section in my Bible is "Jacob Wrestles with God." Yours probably says something similar if it has a title added for clarity by the translators. The reason this title is given for clarity is because this section of Scripture contains what scholars call a theophany, meaning an appearance of God or a preincarnate appearance of Christ. There are several of these in the Old Testament. Don't let those terms confuse you. Let me break them down.

Theophany sounds complicated, but let's break the word in half to make it simpler. Theos is the Greek word for "God." Phany is the Greek word for "appearance or manifestation." So theophany very literally means a "God appearance or manifestation." However, John 1:18 (NIV) says, "No one has ever seen God, but the one and only Son, who is Himself God and is in closest relationship with the Father, has made Him known." If the New Testament claims no one has ever seen God, then how could Jacob have had a "God appearance" moment in the Old Testament? Jacob didn't see the fullness of God Himself. No one can do that and live this side of heaven.

Jacob saw Jesus, the person of the Trinity that we *can* see and still live. Always remember that Jesus is eternal. He always was, always is, and always will be. Christ was the form God took when He appeared as a being to people in the Old Testament. When people say that *theophanies* in the Old Testament are preincarnate appearances of Christ, they simply mean they are appearances of Christ before He physically came to earth in the body of a human. Pre means "before," so if you break the word incarnate in half, in is from the Latin "into," and carnate is from the Latin word where we get our word carnal, or flesh. Put all that together, and "preincarnate appearance of Christ" reads literally, "the before in-flesh Christ." That big intimidating word just means Christ appeared as the visual of God in the Old Testament at times before He ever took on human flesh in the New Testament.

GREAT LENGTHS (JACOB)

In this story of Jacob wrestling with God, the text describes "a man" who wrestled with Jacob until the breaking of the day. The next day, Jacob renamed the location where this event took place. "So Jacob called the name of the place Peniel, saying, 'For I have seen God face to face, and yet my life has been delivered'" (Gen. 32:30). So Jacob realized he was, in fact, wrestling with God, the Son of God.

With the understanding that Jacob was wrestling with God, let's look at the passage. To give a little more context, let me just add that Jacob was about to have to encounter his brother Esau, from whom he stole the firstborn birthright by trickery. Esau had vowed to kill Jacob after he stole his birthright (Gen. 27:41). Many years had passed and Jacob was about to encounter his brother for the first time since all of that went down. To make matters worse, he heard that Esau was coming to meet him with four hundred men (Gen. 32:6).

Jacob became full of fear and anxiety upon receiving this news. He knew on one hand that the inheritance and promises of God were rightfully his own, but on the other hand, he knew he had run ahead of God and obtained them dishonestly and was terrified that he was going to get what was coming to him. He was afraid Esau would try to kill him, his wives, his children, his servants, and his animals. So Jacob decided to try to appease Esau and sent waves of gifts of livestock ahead of himself as peace offerings for his brother. Jacob hoped by the time Esau met him, Esau would be satisfied with all the peace offering gifts and wouldn't kill him and his family. The following verses pick up here:

> The same night he arose and took his two wives, his two female servants, and his eleven children, and crossed the ford of the Jabbok. He took them and sent them across the stream, and everything else that he had. And Jacob was left alone. And a man wrestled with him until the breaking of day. When the man saw that he did not prevail against Jacob, he touched his hip socket, and Jacob's hip was put out of joint as he wrestled with him. Then he said, "Let me go, for the

day has broken." But Jacob said, "I will not let you go unless you bless me." And he said to him, "What is your name?" And he said, "Jacob." Then he said, "Your name shall no longer be called Jacob, but Israel, for you have striven with God and with men, and have prevailed." Then Jacob asked him, "Please tell me your name?" But he said, "Why is it that you ask my name?" And there he blessed him. So Jacob called the name of the place Peniel, saying, "For I have seen God face to face, and yet my life has been delivered." The sun rose upon him as he passed Penuel, limping because of his hip. Therefore to this day, the people of Israel do not eat the sinew of the thigh that is on the hip socket, because he touched the socket of Jacob's hip on the sinew of the thigh. (Gen. 32:22–32)

Why does God choose *this* setting—a wrestling match—as the way He changed Jacob's name to Israel? This is an extremely important name change because this name is the one that will become the description for the entire nation of God's people in the Old Testament. And, as you know, this name has endured even to today as the name of the country on the continent of Asia. So why a name change due to a wrestling match with God? I believe it's because it is a picture of God's work within His chosen. It's so perfect of a picture that God decided to call His people by the name of Israel.

"Jacob" means "heel grabber" or "he cheats" and is a word denoting Jacob's style of trickery to obtain. "Israel," on the other hand, means "strives with God and prevails." Jacob strived or wrestled with God and wrestling is an image of prayer. Likewise, as believers, we wrestle in prayer with God in order to overcome. In other words, the name Israel denotes the idea of becoming an overcomer by wrestling with God in prayer.

Jacob demanded the blessing from God before he would stop wrestling. Years before, God had promised Jacob, not Esau, the blessing of the firstborn and therefore all the covenantal promises of Abraham and Isaac. But instead of waiting on God to bring about the promised plan in His own time, being true to his name, Jacob "tricked" his brother out of the blessing of the firstborn son and took it himself. He jumped ahead of God and took the matter upon himself. Jacob was now full of fear and anxiety as he thought about the possibility that his brother would kill him and his family because of his trickery. He was anxious, worried, and finally reaching the end of himself. He persistently wrestled with God throughout the night to let him keep the blessing He had promised him long ago. Only now was he at the end of himself with no other resources within himself to fix it. Only God could redeem the situation. This was the purest place to be.

It's interesting that God wrestled with Jacob all through the night. The almighty, powerful God who could just say the word and win the battle valued the process more than the win. So He stayed and wrestled all night with Jacob. Finally, when enough was enough, the Scriptures say He simply "touched" Jacob's hip, pulling it out of joint. Still, Jacob clung hard to God, pleading for the blessing. It's as if God finally looked at Jacob and said, "Ah, you finally realize it is Me you have to cling to in order to prevail in My plans for you." And at that point, He changed Jacob's name to Israel as a reminder that only when we strive with God, can we prevail in His plan.

Therefore God made Esau's heart soft toward Jacob, and the reunion was tearful and joyous the next day. A true miracle. The blessing was secured for Jacob, whose name was now Israel.

When we think about prayer as wrestling, this story makes a lot of sense. Prayer is never easy. Most Christians I talk to feel inadequate in this area. They feel intimidated by prayer and often feel like they aren't doing it "right," as if there are rules for how to pray. But, truly, there isn't one right or wrong way. Prayer is simply the process of forming the habit of coming to God. At first it feels odd. But over time, there's a familiarity with praying, as the "rules" of prayer fade, and you find freedom to make it your own unique relationship with God. In prayer we find freedom to be the truest version of ourselves. He knows all of our secrets and situations anyway, so we can come to Him in confession, sorrow, worry, or frustration to allow Him to take the weight off our shoulders. And we can know that through prayer we will receive mercy and grace and power to move forward in a new way. We can wrestle with Him through seemingly impossible situations and especially through the process of overcoming our anxieties and fears. In fact, prayer is the prescription for anxiety. Philippians 4:6–7 (NIV) says: "Do not be anxious about anything but in every situation, [by what?] by prayer and petition, with thanksgiving, present your requests to God. And [then] the peace of God, which transcends all understanding, will guard your hearts and your minds in Christ Jesus."

We can struggle with Him through the uniqueness of each of our hang ups and tendencies. We can cry out to Him throughout the night to intervene in our circumstances. We can joyously praise Him in all things because we know everything is either ordained or allowed by His hand for an ultimate good. We can go to Him pleading for direction or confirmation. Ultimately, if we are striving with God, we are not stagnant. We may not see it until hindsight, but when we strive with God in prayer, He is working in us in ways we may not be aware of and bringing us closer to His heart. We are a people who strive with God and prevail.

He named His people Israel. And we Gentiles get to be grafted into the people of Israel too. You know what Jesus called His house in the New Testament? "My house shall be called a house of prayer" (Matt. 21:13). Jesus didn't say His house would be called a house of good preaching or a house of Bible study or a house of talent or a house of materially successful people. Some of those things, like Bible study and good teaching, are good and necessary things to our spiritual maturity, but He ultimately described His house as a house of prayer—not the regimented kind of prayer full of legalistic rules—but the kind of prayer that creates a well formed habit of coming to Him all throughout the day. I think forming this habit looks different for everyone. But habit breeds a bond of intimacy that cannot be duplicated in any other way. Tie a string around your wrist to remind you, or buy a ring that prompts you to pray every time you see it. Set a reminder on your phone that will buzz multiple times a day. Do whatever you have to do to get yourself into a habit of coming to Him. But give yourself grace. If you miss your reminders one day, just pick up or try something different the next day. Connecting with God through prayer is important enough to make an intentional habit out of it.

In order to describe prayer, Jesus told a parable to give us a visual:

One day Jesus was praying in a certain place. When he finished, one of his disciples said to him, "Lord, teach us to pray, just as John taught his disciples." He said to them, "When you pray, say:
 'Father, hallowed be your name, your kingdom come. Give us each day our daily bread. Forgive us our sins, for we also forgive everyone who sins against us. And lead us not into temptation.'
" Then Jesus said to them, "Suppose you have a friend, and you go to him at midnight and say, 'Friend, lend me three loaves of bread; a friend of mine on a journey has come to me, and I have no food to offer him.' And suppose the one inside answers, 'Don't bother me. The door is already locked, and my children and I are in bed. I can't get up and give you anything.' I tell you, even though he will not get up and give you the bread because of friendship, yet because of your shameless audacity he will surely get up and give you as much as you need.

"So I say to you: Ask and it will be given to you; seek and you will find; knock and the door will be opened to you. For everyone who asks receives; the one who seeks finds; and to the one who knocks, the door will be opened.

"Which of you fathers, if your son asks for a fish, will give him a snake instead? Or if he asks for an egg, will give him a scorpion? If you then, though you are evil, know how to give good gifts to your children, how much more will your Father in heaven give the Holy Spirit to those who ask him!" (Luke 11:1–13 NIV; see also Luke 18:1–8 on prayer)

Note the last line that says, "How much more will your Father in heaven give the Holy Spirit to those who ask Him!" Ask the Lord for an extra measure of the Holy Spirit to help you form a habit of coming to Him. It is the Holy Spirit Who forms in us pure desires and helps us grow in prayer.

I had a personal trainer one time. She kept harping to me about the importance of stretching. I hate stretching. She kept telling me about how studies are finding even more benefits to stretching than we ever knew before. I told her it just felt like a waste of time. I would much rather be doing cardio and burning calories. Finally, she said, "Look, I believe in stretching so much that I'm going to tell you if you only have time for one or the other on any given day, choose stretching." Stretching is to the body as prayer is to spiritual wellness. If any of you are athletes, you know that if you neglect stretching, you stay inflexible, get more injuries, and hit a wall in your progress. If we don't form a habit of prayer, we will likewise stay spiritually rigid and inflexible, and we will injure and stagnate our growth and progress.

I'm going to tell you something that might be controversial, but I believe it to be true. Just like the personal trainer told me, "If you only have time for one or the other on any given day, choose stretching," I'm going to tell you the same about prayer versus Bible study. If you only have time for one or the other one a given day, choose a time of focused prayer. Why? Because our hearts are so prone to wander. Our hearts need constant connection to our Maker or, before we know it, we'll have wandered away. Prayer keeps our hearts connected. Make a habit of going to God. That's all prayer is—the habit of going to God. Sometimes it's completely focused, set aside time. Other times it's while we are driving or cleaning the house. Of course, make time for both prayer *and* Bible study, but if schedules don't go as planned one day and you only have time to focus on one or the other in your set aside time, choose prayer. The mind can recall and remember Scripture for long amounts of time. The heart, though, is ever prone to wander. It *needs* the constant connection. However, please don't take what I just said and let it be a license to replace Bible study with prayer. That's not the point. If you do that for more than just occasionally, you'll find your prayers will likewise go stagnant. The point is just to say that I see the church putting such a heavy emphasis on Bible study but very little emphasis on prayer. Too many Christians feel inadequate in prayer because they rarely set aside personal time for it. And remember what Jesus said: "My house shall be called a house of *prayer*" (Matt. 21:13, emphasis mine). It's foundational for an intimate walk with Him.

There's a bonus to prayer too. Prayer infuses our Bible study over time, carrying the effects further to our spiritual body, just like stretching infuses our cardio over time, carrying the effects further to our physical body. Now that we have made the parallel between stretching and prayer, listen to some of the benefits of stretching from Doctor of Physical Therapy Justine Cosman, and make your own spiritual connections. Stretching:

1. Reduces muscle tension (can also reduce feelings of stress)
2. Increases flexibility and range of movement in the joints
3. Enhances muscular coordination
4. Increases circulation of blood, carrying more nutrients to the various body parts
5. Increases optimism and energy levels resulting from the increased circulation
6. Aides in lowering cholesterol to avoid heart disease and the hardening of arteries
7. Improves your posture[45]

Did you make any parallels between the effects of stretching and the effects of prayer? It's much better to have both stretching *and* cardio, and both prayer *and* Bible study. They work best hand in hand. But it is the foundation of prayer (the habit of coming to Him in conversation) that brings the lessons in the Bible to life, circulating them to your heart and mind through the Spirit. And sometimes while reading the Bible, we find ourselves drawn to prayer. They work best hand in hand, but prayer is of paramount importance in taking the Word deeper into our souls and making application.

When we wrestle with God in prayer, we realize the truth of our own inadequacy, and by persisting in prayer, we also find strength and sustenance to endure our circumstances with hope. And eventually, when we have overcome, we will be given a new name. God has a thing for giving new names. He tends to identify with how we finish rather than with our failures along the way. "To him who overcomes, to him I will give some of the hidden manna, and I will give him a white stone, and a new name written on the stone which no one knows but he who receives it" (Rev. 2:17 NASB).

The "white stone" mentioned in this verse is most likely an allusion to the ancient Roman athletic games. They would award victors white stones with their names inscribed on them. This stone with your name on it served as your "ticket" into a special awards banquet for everyone who overcame their opponent.[46] Jesus promises a victory celebration in heaven to everyone who overcomes (1 Cor. 9:24–27). Wrestle with God in prayer and overcome. He may not always answer like we expect, but He will use the persistent wrestling with Him to do the incredible in us and in our circumstances. "Fight the good fight of the faith" (1 Tim. 6:12).

Jacob's Ladder

Jacob's Ladder is the title of several movies and TV shows. Get on your favorite movie app sometime and search "Jacob's Ladder." You'll find lots and lots of results. There seems to be a fascination with the idea of Jacob's ladder among movie makers. But did you know that the concept actually came from the Bible? It's true. Many years before God changed Jacob's name to Israel, He appeared to him in a dream:

> Taking one of the stones of the place, [Jacob] put it under his head and lay down in that place to sleep. And he dreamed, and behold, there was a ladder set up on the earth, and the top of it reached to heaven. And behold, the angels of God were ascending and descending on it! And behold, the Lord stood above it and said, "I am the Lord, the God of Abraham your father and the God of Isaac. The land on which you lie I will give to you and to your offspring. Your offspring shall be like the dust of the earth, and you shall spread abroad to the west and to the east and to the north and to the south, and in you and your offspring shall all the families of the earth be blessed. Behold, I am with you and will keep you wherever you go, and will bring you back to this land. For I will not leave you until I have done what I have promised you." Then Jacob awoke from his sleep and said, "Surely the Lord is in this place, and I did not know it." And he was afraid and said, "How awesome is this place! This is none other than the house of God, and this is the gate of heaven." (Gen. 28:10–17)

This experience no doubt encouraged Jacob that God was intimately involved with him for the formation of His chosen nation. The promises mentioned in the dream concerned the *offspring*, the *land* of Israel, and *blessing* for the world through his offspring. The promises in this dream are still being fulfilled in many ways today, but they ultimately pointed forward to Christ. Jesus Christ was *the ultimate offspring* foreshadowed through the line of Jacob/Israel; Jesus will reign as king over the *land* of Israel during the millennium from His throne in Jerusalem; and through Jesus (Israel's offspring) all the families of the earth will be *blessed*.

After Jacob awoke from the dream, he decided to rename the location to commemorate the dream. The name of the city was originally called "Luz," but Jacob renamed the city "Bethel." Luz means "separation," and bethel means "house of God."[47] The ladder in his dream was a sort of bridge between heaven and earth. The dream assumes that there was separation before the bridge or ladder was revealed in the dream but now the people of the earth could have access to the house of God. The bridge or ladder is a picture of Jesus. Jesus is the one that built a ladder between heaven and earth for us. It is only through Christ that we gain access to the throne room of God. We were once "separated" (Luz) from God in our sin, but Christ made a ladder of atoning blood (blood that came through the line of Jacob/Israel) that now connects us to be part of the "house of God" (Bethel)!

At the beginning of Jesus's earthly ministry in the New Testament, He referenced this dream. Many Jews in the time of Jesus knew the Old Testament so well that a teacher did not have to explain the entire story in order to let his audience know what he was talking about. One common line from a story could be quoted, and everyone knew what they were referring to. Listen to Jesus's words at the very end of this passage:

> Nathanael said to Him, "How do You know me?" Jesus answered him, "Before Philip called you, when you were under the fig tree, I saw you." Nathanael answered Him, "Rabbi, You are the Son of God! You are the King of Israel!" Jesus answered him, "Because I said to you, I saw you under the fig tree, do you believe? You will see greater things than these." And He said to him, "Truly, truly, I say to you, you will see heaven opened, and the angels of God ascending and descending on the Son of Man." (John 1:48–51)

Did you catch that? It was the same language used of the angels ascending and descending in the dream of Jacob's ladder. After his dream, Jacob immediately recognized that the place where the end of the ladder had rested on earth in the city of Bethel must be the "gate of heaven." To Jacob, the place—the city of Bethel—was the "gate of heaven" (Gen. 28:17). But when Jesus came, He was saying the angels would be ascending and descending on *Him*, not on a place. He was the new gate of heaven. Jesus was *the* way to heaven. Jesus even calls Himself the gate in John 10:9 (NIV), "I am the gate; whoever enters through Me will be saved. They will come in and go out, and find pasture." Jesus was trying to communicate to the people of Israel by using every means of familiar language to them to show Himself as the Messiah they had been waiting for. He goes to great lengths to woo us to Himself. Do you let yourself hear it?

CHAPTER 10

Not Forgotten
(Jacob & the Twelve Tribes of Israel)

YOU'VE LIKELY NOTICED A fad in America where you call your family your "tribe." I guess fads really do come around again and again, because that's exactly what the twelve families springing from Jacob's twelve sons called themselves—*tribes*! It was through these twelve sons' families that a literal nation called Israel formed. Remember Jacob's name was changed to Israel. So very simply put, the nation of Israel formed through the twelve tribes or families that came from Jacob's sons.

Can you imagine? A nation made up of one big family reunion! If any of you have a large family, you know families can get complicated at times. You might even look at some of the members of your family and humorously think, "How in the world can I be related to *them*?" My friend Tammy Whitehurst often says, "Families are like pecan pie—a whole lot of nuts held together by a firm foundation!" That sounds about right, doesn't it?

Have no doubt, the family of Jacob was no different. They were a bunch of nuts held together by a firm foundation! There was quarreling and jealousy and eventually wars between one another. I guess that just goes to show that life with people is messy, no matter where you are or in which generation you live.

We see that life with people is messy, even in the church today. I've known people who have had conflict with *a* church and have walked away from *the* church entirely. That's kind of like having conflict with one family member but walking away from the entire family instead. Conflict just happens; so do misunderstandings, misjudgments, misinterpretations, which all lead to conflict. We shouldn't run from conflict or discount anyone who causes conflict. Truth be told, we've all had our share of a little drama that was our fault, haven't we? Instead, why not look at conflict as an opportunity for grace? Grace is undeserved favor, and it is the heart of the gospel. Grace is what can truly change a person from the inside out.

Here's what has helped me. This is going to sound absurdly simple—but start viewing people this way, and how you handle relational situations will change. View people as image-bearers of God. Genesis 1:27 says human beings were "created in God's image." Even those of the world who are not saved still bear His image just by the very nature of being a human being. This concept is made clearer by Matthew 22:17–21:

> [The Pharisees said,] "Tell us, then, what you think. Is it lawful to pay taxes to Caesar, or not?" But Jesus, aware of their malice, said, "Why put me to the test, you hypocrites? Show me the coin for the tax." And they brought him a denarius. And Jesus said to them, "Whose likeness and inscription is this?" They said, "Caesar's." Then he said to them, "Therefore render to Caesar the things that are Caesar's, and to God the things that are God's."

In the last line, Jesus was playing on the fact that human beings bear God's image. We belong to God, and we owe ourselves to Him, whether we choose to give our lives to Him or not.

A little later, Jesus taught that this concept spans even further than that. Since humans are made in the image of God, Jesus explained that how we treat people is how we are treating God: "Truly I tell you, whatever you did for one of the least of these brothers and sisters of mine, you did for Me" (Matthew 25:40 NIV).

Would you have trouble ripping up a painting that your child worked so hard to create? Well, each of us are God's workmanship (Eph. 2:10). Would you have trouble trashing a Bible? Well, we are products of His spoken Word (Gen. 1–2).

We wear name-brand clothing bearing the name of a famous person, and we pay inflated amounts of money for these items. Would you have more trouble tearing up your name-brand clothing or tearing down your sister or brother in Christ behind their back? There have been seasons of my life when I would confess to you that I valued my name-brand clothing more because it touched my pocketbook and my popularity.

I had a perspective shift when I started realizing that whatever I do to even the least of people, I was doing to Christ Himself. How can Christ have done so much for me and then I treat the ones that bear His image poorly in return? I can't control how the other person acts. But I can control how I act. I'm only going to have to answer for how I acted. The other side of the equation isn't on me. There have often been times when I would act like a brat in order to try to manipulate the other person to change. But the truth is, my responsibility is to be who I know God is asking me to be, regardless of how the other person acts.

So maybe stop right now or get in a space alone with God today if you're having conflict with someone. Read Jesus's parable of the unforgiving servant (Matt. 18:21–35). This passage nails it. You won't regret it. Ask Him to give you strength to lay down your own "rights" in the situation and then ask Him to show you how to show the other person the same grace you first learned from Him.

Jesus said, "Do not judge, or you too will be judged. For in the same way you judge others, you will be judged, and with the measure you use, it will be measured to you. Why do you look at the speck of sawdust in your brother's eye and pay no attention to the plank in your own eye?"

(Matt. 7:1–3). There have been times in conflict where I have felt 100 percent innocent and right and would even tell you there wasn't a plank in my eye. But in some of those very same scenarios, I later learned new information about the other person's perspective that I did not know at the time, and as I reflected on the situation in hindsight, I was ashamed of my judgment. It's never ours to judge. It's always right to reconcile and extend grace and mercy, just as Christ has done for us. Giving grace and mercy isn't weakness; it is strength. Take a second and reflect on these two Scriptures:

> Serve one another humbly in love. For the entire law is fulfilled in keeping this one command: "Love your neighbor as yourself." If you bite and devour each other, watch out or you will be destroyed by each other. So I say, walk by the Spirit, and you will not gratify the desires of the flesh. (Gal. 5:13–16 NIV)

> But grow in the grace and knowledge of our Lord and Savior Jesus Christ. (2 Pet. 3:18)

Twelve Tribes of Israel—Foundations for Understanding

Because the livelihood of each family in biblical times was often sustained by flocks, herds, and crops, the ever-growing families of the sons of Jacob (Israel) couldn't all live in one city or area once they were in the land God had promised them. They had to spread out if they were going to allow their livestock and crops to thrive. So they divided the land among the tribal lines or family lines.

If you're using a study Bible, flip back to the maps section. Most likely there will be a map showing the land possessed by each of the twelve tribes of Israel. You will notice that there are twelve sections of land divided out, each labeled with the name of a son or grandson of Israel. Here's the list:

1. Reuben
2. Simeon
3. Levi
4. Judah
5. Issachar
6. Zebulun
7. Dan
8. Naphtali
9. Gad
10. Asher
11. Joseph (later Ephraim and Manasseh)
12. Benjamin

Before Jacob (Israel) died, he was reunited with his favorite son, Joseph, whom he thought was dead but was actually alive living successfully in Egypt (more on that in the next chapter). Jacob decided to give Joseph the firstborn inheritance rather than Reuben who was the actual firstborn, because Reuben had disappointed him. The firstborn's inheritance was a double portion. Jacob therefore gave Joseph a double portion of inheritance by blessing Joseph's two kids with the rights of full sons of Jacob (Israel). Ephraim and Manasseh would then have just as much right as any other son of Jacob in the confederacy.

But if Joseph's double portion gives each of his sons a full portion, that makes thirteen tribes, right? That's right. Here's the compensation: The tribe of Levi was assigned a special task by the Lord to perform the religious duties among all the tribes, so the tribe of Levi got no unified allotment of land (Josh. 13:33; Num. 18). God did assign them places to live, but they were scattered in forty-eight different places throughout all of the tribes so they could adequately minister to each (Josh. 21:41). Upon his deathbed, Jacob had previously prophesied that Levi's descendants would be scattered throughout Israel (Gen. 49:7), and this came to pass when God appointed the Levites as the priestly tribe. Since they were religious servants, scattering them among everyone made them accessible to everyone.

I've explained all of this to paint a picture that will make this next part make sense. There are two necessary tribes to associate with specific roles when studying the Bible: the tribe of Levi and the tribe of Judah. The tribe of Levi's role was the priesthood. When you hear the term Levitical priesthood, it simply means "the priesthood of the tribe of Levi." Aaron was descended from Levi and became the first high priest of Israel. The whole tribe of Levi was designated as the priestly class and was in charge of holy ministrations like orchestrating animal sacrifices for the people's sins. If you're reading through the New Testament one day and it mentions that someone was a high priest, that means they were from the tribe of Levi. So only if someone was from the tribe of Levi did he have rights to perform priestly duties if called upon to do so.

The most intriguing example of this to me is John the Baptist. Did you know that John the Baptist was from the tribe of Levi? We know this because Luke 1 records that his father Zechariah was performing his priestly duties in the temple when an angel of the Lord appeared to him, foretelling that his son John would be filled with the Holy Spirit from birth and would turn many of the children of Israel to the Lord. He was commissioned and approved by the Lord.

John the Baptist (John the baptizer) went around baptizing people. The baptism he performed played off the purification rituals of the priesthood (Lev. 15:13), which powerfully symbolized repentance. Repent, be washed, and start fresh. On one occasion John said, "I baptize you with water for repentance, but He Who is coming after me is mightier than I, whose sandals I am not worthy to carry. He will baptize you with the Holy Spirit and fire" (Matt. 3:11). In other words, John the Baptist recognized that water was only a symbol and only had power to cleanse the outside. Jesus would be able to lead us to repentance and *truly* cleanse us from the inside out through the work of the Holy Spirit. True change is always from the inside out; trying to fix the outside so the inside might match is futile. We need the help of the Holy Spirit to wash the inside so the outside will begin to reflect the inner change. "For out of the abundance of the heart, his mouth speaks" (Luke 6:45). The inside effects the outside, not the other way around. So John recognized Jesus as the One who would bring about a greater baptism.

John the Baptist's Levitical, priestly heritage is also intriguing to me because the Scriptures say that when John saw Jesus coming toward him, John would cry out for all to hear, "'Behold, the Lamb of God who takes away the sin of the world! This is He of whom I said, 'After me comes a Man who ranks before me, because He was before me.' I myself did not know Him, but for this purpose I came baptizing with water, that He might be revealed to Israel'" (John 1:29–31). John calls Jesus the "Lamb of God who takes away the sin of the world!" It was the Levitical priesthood's role to approve the lamb selections for Passover. John the Baptist, being from the tribe of Levi, was officially approving the ultimate Passover Lamb who would take away the sin of the world. And it just so happens that Jesus's crucifixion happened exactly when the Passover lambs were being slaughtered. The Feast of Passover is the most important feast to the Jewish people. God sovereignly and perfectly orchestrated all of this in order to convince the Jewish people of their Messiah, yet they couldn't see it. But we can see it, and we can continue to share with them how Jesus perfectly fulfills all of their Scriptures, their feasts, and everything in between. It's the time of the Gentiles right now, but the time of the Jews is coming again. Let us prepare the way for the Lord in that.

The other tribal role we need to highlight is the role of the tribe of Judah. In the Old Testament God designated the tribe of Judah as the tribe from which kings would come. Sometimes Israel followed this when choosing their kings and sometimes not. Israel divided at one point and had a northern kingdom and southern kingdom, so obviously in that era all the kings weren't from the southern tribe of Judah. But the God-ordained kings were always from this tribe. The famous King David was from the tribe of Judah, and the prophecies concerning the Messiah who would one day be King of all denoted that He would come from the tribe of Judah. Jesus descended from David in the tribe of Judah and will one day be recognized as King of all. Every knee will bow and every tongue will confess that Jesus Christ is Lord, to the glory of the Father (Phil. 2:10–11; Rom. 14:11).

On his deathbed, when Jacob (Israel) prophetically blessed his son Judah (Gen. 49:9), he referred to him and his tribe as a lion's cub and a lion. And then, referring to Jesus, Revelation 5:5 says, "And one of the elders said to me, 'Weep no more; behold, *the lion of the tribe of Judah*, the Root of David, has conquered, so that He can open the scroll and its seven seals'" (emphasis mine). Verses like these are why we hear people call Christ the "Lion of the tribe of Judah." They say in Jesus's first coming, He came in like a lamb ready for slaughter. But at His final coming, He will come like a lion. The church will have been raptured by that point, but we will witness Him roaring like a magnificent lion with vengeance to defeat evil and our enemies on the earth. At that point He will set up His thousand-year reign on earth as King (the millennium), and believers from all generations since creation will reign with Him.

The Ten Lost Tribes of Israel

One time when I was about to fly to South Carolina to attend a conference, I started praying that God would let me have a conversation with a Jewish person. I don't know why I prayed that or why it's even a desire of my heart, other than the more I study the Bible, the more I see how much Jewish heritage we have as Christians. God chose them. He sent Jesus through them. They may have hardened hearts toward Christ right now during the current time (the age of the Gentiles), but their time is coming again. It will be a time in which they come to salvation because of the foundation Christ laid for them through us. I believe that. I think we will be one again. So I guess that's why I pray crazy things like that when I go on trips.

Anyway, I arrived at the conference and one of the first bits of news I heard was that the conference leaders had pulled in a last-minute musical guest as a special treat for us. The last-minute guest was singer-songwriter Marty Goetz, a Jewish man. I was so excited. God had answered my prayer. Marty Goetz grew up in New York and eventually came to see Jesus as the fulfillment of Scripture, so He put his faith in Jesus and started a full-time ministry of music to honor the Lord. To this day there's just something about his song "Sanctuary" that stirs my heart.

They say when a Gentile comes to salvation it's a great thing, but when a Jew comes to salvation it's a miraculous thing. They have all the Jewish history, customs, and background, and when their eyes are opened to how Jesus fulfills all of it both poetically and literally, their passion fans into flame. That was the case with Marty. I know this because we all had breakfast with him the next morning, and we could very obviously see the passion exuding from him as he talked about this with us.

I truly thought God had completely answered my prayer by sending a Jewish man to be our musician at the conference. And if that's all there was, He would have answered it in my eyes. But there was more to come.

I got on the plane to come home and sat in my assigned seat. I secretly hoped the vacant seat next to me would stay empty because I was tired from the week. But a middle-aged man plopped down next to me and started searching for his seat belt.

So then, naturally, I formed another hope that this gentleman wouldn't want to talk all the way home. I didn't want to be rude, but I was tired. Next thing I knew, the man started a conversation with me. I decided nothing is ever a coincidence, so I mustered up the energy to return conversation and let the Lord lead it wherever He wanted it to go. We shared the typical answers to questions like "Where are you from?" "What do you do?" "How many kids do you have?" We had talked for about twenty minutes. Finally the conversation lulled, and I thought, "Nice. . ."

He looked down for about thirty or forty seconds in silence, staring at his phone. Then he popped back with, "I just feel like I'm supposed to tell you I'm a Jew."

I was like, "What? No way!" And, as you can imagine, the conversation ended up lasting the entire two-hour flight home.

Turns out my new friend had no idea he was a Jew his entire life until a few years prior. He said his grandparents had faced immense persecution, moved to America, and decided to start fresh without blatantly telling people they were Jewish. That way, if no one in America knew their family was Jewish, they wouldn't be persecuted.

The Holocaust, persecution, enslavement, and intermingling with other nations are probably just some of the reasons Jewish people have neglected their heritage. Many Jewish people don't have any idea anymore what tribe of Israel they descend from.

But there's another reason there are "lost tribes" today. Of course it's more complicated than how I am going to explain it, but it will give you the nutshell, and if you're interested in knowing more, you can search it out yourself.

The land was divided among the twelve tribes of Israel. The entire kingdom of Israel began fighting and was divided between the north and the south. There were ten tribes split to the north and two tribes split to the south. The southern two tribes were Benjamin and Judah. There were ten in the north against two in the south.

Since Israel was now split in two and both the north *and* the south couldn't go by the name of Israel, in the latter parts of the Old Testament we see new names start to emerge for each of the two portions. This makes the Old Testament a little confusing if you don't know this background. The north began to be called the "house of Israel" (sometimes just Israel, but usually "house of" denotes the north is being referred to). The north was also called "Ephraim" at times, which was one of the sons of Joseph who was a recipient of a piece of the double portion. Obviously the tribe of Ephraim was significant in the north or they wouldn't have allowed his name to describe all of them.

The south, on the other hand, began to be called "Judah." There were more tribes than just Judah in the south, but for one reason or another, the entire south took their identification as Judah.

So these are the names after the split: the northern tribes were referred to as the "House of Israel," "Israel," or "Ephraim," and the southern tribes were referred to as "Judah."

God warned both the north and the south through His prophets about various sins, areas of disobedience, and idolatries within each of them. When they didn't heed His warnings, He allowed them to go into captivity to other nations. The Lord decided to allow the north to go into captivity to Assyria as a season of discipline to show He had withdrawn His hand. He did the same thing with the south, except He used Babylon to take the south into captivity.

The Lord withdrew His hand as discipline because they did not heed His warnings. Have you ever felt God withdraw His hand from you because you weren't heeding His warnings? I have. I was meddling in a very gray area for me. Some would say it was okay, and some would say it is wrong. God was personally telling me it was wrong for me. Even though I could feel the Spirit's conviction regarding the subject, I wanted to continue dabbling more than I wanted to stop. So what did I do? In all my God-given smartness, I justified rather than listened. I found what I felt were loopholes in Scripture and stood on those rather than the words that were clear. I purposely avoided the Scriptures I knew would convict me. I did this for about four months. Finally I encountered what I somehow knew was one of the last warnings from the Spirit I would get on the matter before God would start taking action. I was torn.

Forgotten Faith

Would I surrender and lay the situation down, or continue and suffer the consequences and maybe even lose the anointing I had felt for so long from the Lord? I became terrified of losing the Lord's anointing and ultimately asked for His help to surrender. After that prayer God shifted the situation and provided me a way out. Then He immediately began to show me the vastness of my error and began revealing things I had stubbornly made myself blind to. I was broken and sorry as I fell on my knees and cried before the Lord for all the wasted time. Every Sunday at church for the next couple of months, the Spirit flooded back in so strongly that I would cry out of gratitude for second chances through almost the entire time of worship. The amount of grace that came into my life was unprecedented. It was a bittersweet time, but a much-needed time. For the first time during that season, I believe I truly came to understand a new depth of grace.

I tremble now, knowing how close I was to experiencing God withdraw His hand. I wasn't just failing to heed His warnings, I had almost totally allowed myself to become hardened to hearing His conviction at all. There were times where I would tell myself, "See? It doesn't feel wrong. I don't feel convicted." But that was only because I had quenched the Spirit so much that I wasn't able to hear Him anymore on the subject. The last warning I received broke through the hardness of my heart and awakened in me a moment of choice. It was a clear fork in the road, and I knew it. It was the last chance to divert back onto His path without real and undeniable consequences.

If you are dabbling in an area of conviction, please don't let it take the time it took me. Don't be like northern and southern Israel who both went into captivity because they would not heed His warnings. Believe God is in control of all things, whether you agree to it or not. He will get His way, with or without you. But I will tell you, now that I know what the possibility of losing it feels like, God's hand on my life has become worth far more than anything else. You won't lose your salvation if you don't lay that thing down that He's asking you to lay down, but I promise, there will come a time when you are so very sorry if you don't. It will break your heart when you realize everything you lost. It's fun at first, but sin always steals in the end.

God was long-suffering with His people despite their blatant rebellion. He continued to warn His people through prophets even while they were in captivity. Over the course of time, the south was able to come back from captivity, but the north never did, even to this day.

Since the southern tribes were the only ones that came back from captivity before Christ's birth, most of the people mentioned in the New Testament who identify with tribes are from the southern tribes of Benjamin, Judah, or Levi (although the ones from the tribe of Levi were only a partial tribe because this tribe was scattered throughout the twelve tribes in both the north and the south). Occasionally in the New Testament, we will find someone who is recognized to be from a northern tribe, like from the tribe of Asher, for example. The reason for this is because some of the tribes didn't stay loyal to their territories during the disagreements and moved, changing from north to south or vice versa. For the most part, though, the Jews who were involved in the events surrounding Jesus were from the southern tribes, since those who had sided with the north were still in captivity.

Paul, who wrote the majority of the New Testament, was from the tribe of Benjamin (a southern tribe); John the Baptist was from the tribe of Levi (partially a southern tribe); Mary, Joseph, and Jesus were from the tribe of Judah (a southern tribe). Since the southern tribes were referred to collectively as "Judah," the name got shortened and they began to simply be called "Jews." Do you hear the Jew sound in "Judah?" Today, in modern terminology, the term Jew has evolved to encompass everyone descended from the twelve tribes of Israel, lost or found, but it wasn't always that way.

The northern tribes have been in captivity so long that they have probably lost all identity as God's chosen people. They have most likely intermingled with the pagan lifestyle of Assyria, and many probably now have no idea they ever descended from another nation. Whether they know their heritage or not, they are still the "ten lost tribes of Israel," and God has His eyes on them.

The Bible says God will gather the scattered, lost ones of Israel, even from the four corners of the earth (see Jer. 23:3; 31:7–8; 32:37; Isa. 11:11–1, 16). The book of Revelation says that during the end times, 12,000 from *each* tribe will come to Christ and be sealed (see Rev. 7). Romans 11 speaks of God's *future* work in the nation of Israel.

We are starting to see the beginnings of Ezekiel 37 happening even today. This prophecy states that there will be a future regathering of Israel in her land, even though it will start with unbelief. Israel didn't become a nation again until 1948, and now, Jews in increasing numbers from all over the world are moving to Israel. One well-known Jew who recently moved from America to Israel is Joel Rosenberg, a well-known Jewish-Christian author of political thrillers.

Ezekiel 37 predicts that there is supposed to be political and spiritual revival in the land of Israel. We are seeing the political revival already. Just recently the United States took a stand for Israel by moving the embassy from Tel Aviv to Jerusalem, therefore declaring Jerusalem to be the capital of Israel. This was a huge move on the political front for Jews in Israel, and other nations are following the lead of the United States. Israel has been blessed by God with cutting-edge inventions and military power, and many recognize that and desire to be allies with her. Israel is, therefore, rising in favor among the nations.

We are beginning to see spiritual revival, though, as well. When Tom Doyle, author of *Dreams and Visions*, and his wife, JoAnn, return to the United States from their mission work with Uncharted Ministries, they go around telling God-sized stories of what goes on in their mission field. Their mission work is primarily to Muslims and Jews, and they attest to the fact that the number of Muslims and Jews coming to salvation is increasing rapidly like never before. The spiritual activity is stirring among both groups. God is up to something. He is bringing His prophecy to fruition at its appointed time, and the ten lost tribes will be found.

The Time of Jacob's Trouble

If you've heard much about prison ministry, you've probably heard some pretty awesome stories. There's just something about our sins finally catching up to us that gives opportunity for a true turnaround. It's a fork in the road where we can choose to stay the same and set the record player on repeat, or we can choose to turn around and walk in the direction with God that we were designed for all along. That's what "the time of Jacob's trouble" is supposed to bring about for the Jewish people, but it's going to be a hard road. The phrase "the time of Jacob's trouble" comes from a prophesy in Jeremiah 30:3–7 (NKJV):

> "For behold, the days are coming," says the Lord, "that I will bring back from captivity My people Israel and Judah," says the Lord. "And I will cause them to return to the land that I gave to their fathers, and they shall possess it." Now these are the words the Lord spoke concerning Israel and Judah. For thus says the Lord: "We have heard a voice of trembling, of fear, and not of peace. Ask now, and see, whether a man is ever in labor with child? So why do I see every man with his hands on his loins like a woman in labor, and all faces turned pale? Alas! For that day is great, so that none is like it; and it is the time of Jacob's trouble, but he shall be saved out of it."

The "time of Jacob's trouble" is another term for the great tribulation.[48] Let me refresh your memory with a chart of the order of end-times events:

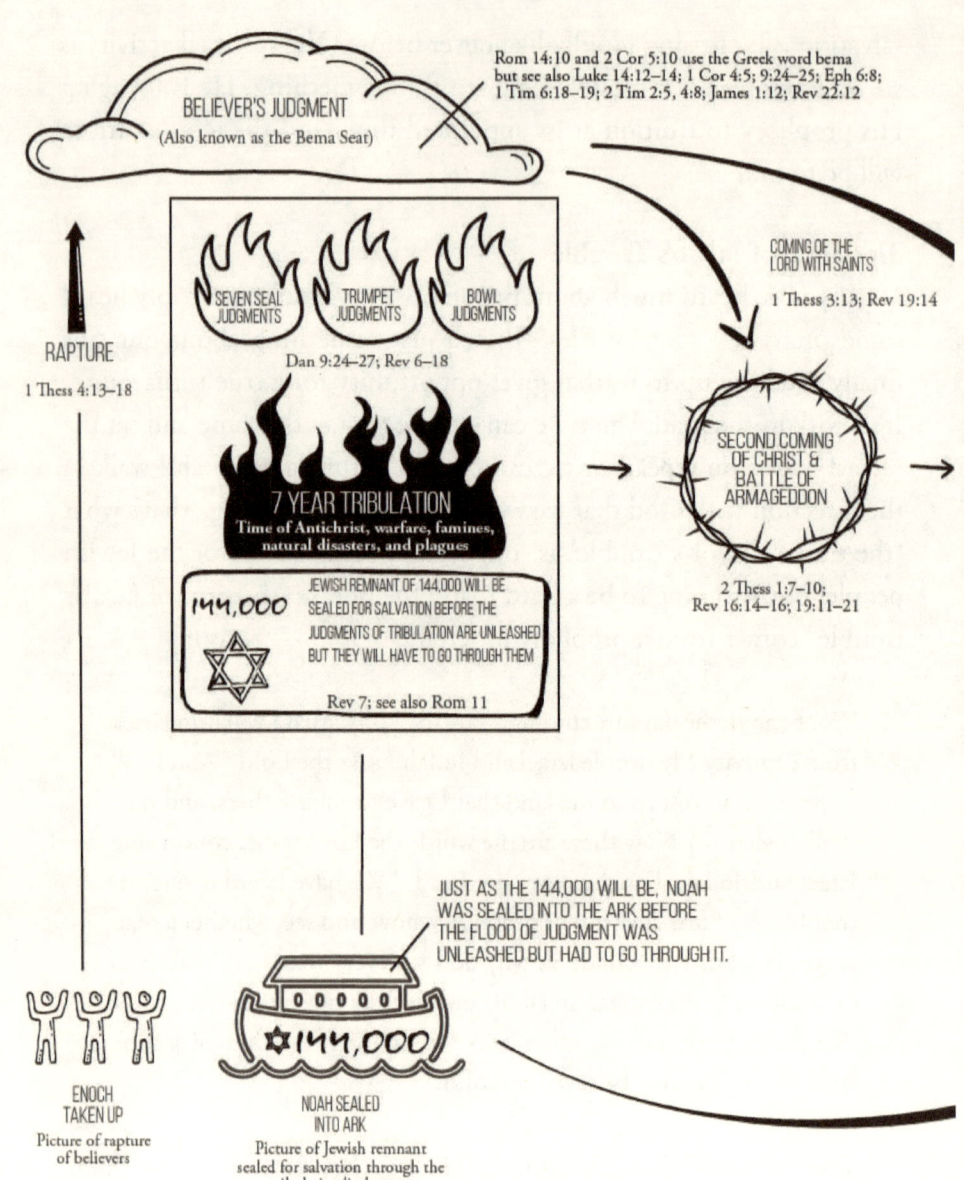

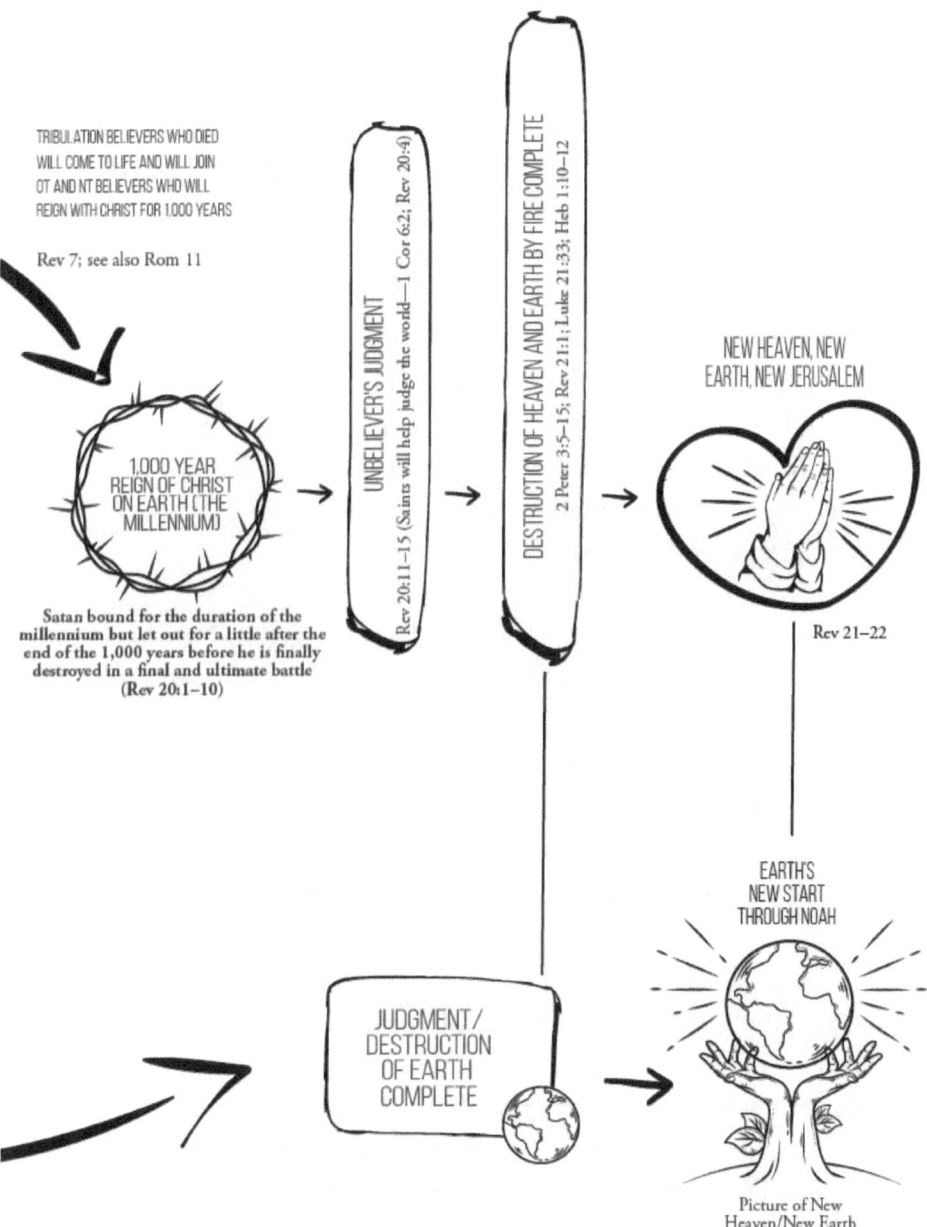

Note: These are not all the Scripture references that exist on each topic. A study on each topic individually would prove beneficial. Please also note that this chart depicts the pretribulation rapture belief, of which I believe and find the most support for, but it could easily be modified to also support the midtribulation rapture belief. The midtribulation view works when we consider that the great tribulation doesn't begin until halfway through the seven-year tribulation period—the second half being the most intense of the tribulations by far.

First on the chart comes the rapture of the church. Note that at the rapture, the Lord doesn't return to earth—we meet Him in the air. That's the difference between the rapture and the second coming of Christ. Like many scholars I also take the view that the church will be raptured before the tribulation for many reasons we find in Scripture. But the two most cut and dried reasons are (1) the fact that the book of Revelation is written chronologically. The first three chapters mention the church in detail. There is no mention of the church in the book of Revelation after the first three chapters. It is *after* the first three chapters of Revelation that the tribulation and judgments begin to be explained; and (2) various Scriptures attest to the fact that those who believe in Jesus before the tribulation begins are not destined for wrath, and the tribulation is described as wrath:

- "Since, therefore, we have now been justified by His blood, how much more shall we be saved by Him from the wrath of God" (Romans 5:9).
- "Jesus who delivers us from the wrath to come" (1 Thessalonians 1:10).
- "For God has not destined us for wrath, but to obtain salvation through our Lord Jesus Christ" (1 Thessalonians 5:19).

These verses do not say we will be spared from hardship or persecution or trial, but from the wrath of God. Yes, the tribulation period contains the Antichrist, with all his scheming and destruction, but the tribulation period also contains the seven seals, the seven trumpets, and the seven bowls of God's *wrath*. In addition the verses speak to the fact that those who are saved in Christ prior to the tribulation will be spared from the wrath. It is the rapture that will remove believers from the coming wrath on earth. Therefore I believe the church is raptured before the wrath of God occurs, but if we disagree on this point, it's okay. It's not a major point in Christianity. God will give us strength to endure either way it goes.

Second on the chart comes the seven-year tribulation. But the seven-year tribulation has two parts. The second three and a half years of the tribulation will be way more intense than the first three and a half years. Because of its intensity, the second half of the tribulation is called "the great tribulation" or "the time of Jacob's trouble."

In Matthew 24, Jesus described this last three and a half years (the great tribulation) as beginning with the abomination of desolation, spoken of by the prophet Daniel. Since the abomination Daniel spoke of will occur in the temple, we know that the Jews will have finally built the third temple by this moment in time (*Side Note: The Jews of today have already started building the third temple in Israel. The required inside items have been constructed and are being securely stored while they wait to find a way to build the walls at their desired location. Everything is already in motion for the end events to take place*). The beast will be reigning at the time of the great tribulation and will be given power by Satan (Rev. 12:12; 13:1–5). The Antichrist will break his covenant with the Jews and demand to be worshiped in the temple. This is the abomination of desolation (Dan. 9:27; Matt. 24:15; 2 Thess. 2:4). Once this happens the great tribulation will begin. This is the last three and a half years before Christ's second coming.

Jesus said there has never been a day as bad as the days of the great tribulation. Out of mercy God is going to cut the days short for the sake of those who are brought to salvation in Christ during this time. "For then there will be great tribulation, such as has not been from the beginning of the world until now, no, and never will be. And if those days had not been cut short, no human being would be saved. But for the sake of the elect those days will be cut short" (Matt. 24:21–22). During this time the Jews will hide in the wilderness for 1,260 days (approximately the last three and a half years of the tribulation) to try to find relief from the Antichrist (Rev. 12; Dan. 7:25; 13:5–7).

It will be a terrible, terrible time for everyone on the earth, but especially for the Jews. The great tribulation is also called the time of Jacob's trouble because the focus will be on the Jews. The people of God who came to be called Israel (or nowadays called the Jews) were God's first people, so they get firstborn kind of blessing and cursing. The firstborn's inheritance is double. They get double blessing but they also get double cursing (see Isa. 40:1–2; Jer. 16:16–18). As a people group they were given greater revelation from God. The Bible's Old and New Testaments were almost entirely written by Jews. And with greater revelation comes greater responsibility (see Amos 3:2; Luke 12:4). They will be held to a higher accountability.

You might be reading this thinking it sounds so harsh and wondering what the purpose of the tribulation is and especially what the purpose of the great tribulation is. There are several verses that speak to God's purpose in allowing a tribulation time for the Jews and for those who did not accept Christ before the rapture. Here's His purpose in it: to bring an end to wickedness (Isa. 13:9; 24:19–20), encourage every last soul to come to Him for salvation (Rev. 7:1–7), and to completely wipe out the stubborn rebellion of the nation of Israel against Him (Ezek. 20:33–38; Dan. 9:24; 12:7). The intensity of time will refine the people into pure holiness and complete commitment to Him. He will truly be their only hope during that time.

Matthew 24:29–31 continues our chart:

> Immediately after the tribulation of those days, the sun will be darkened, and the moon will not give its light, and the stars will fall from heaven, and the powers of the heavens will be shaken. Then will appear in heaven the sign of the Son of Man, and then all the tribes of the earth will mourn, and they will see the Son of Man coming on the clouds of heaven with power and great glory. And He will send

out His angels with a loud trumpet call, and they will gather His elect from the four winds, from one end of heaven to the other.

According to Revelation 19:11–20:6, when Jesus comes and sends His angels to gather His people together in Israel, this is also the point when the battle of Armageddon is fought. There are many casualties, but not of the Lord's people this time. John's revelation from the Lord says,

> Then I saw an angel coming down from heaven, holding in his hand the key to the bottomless pit and a great chain. And he sealed the dragon, that ancient serpent, who is the devil and Satan, and bound him for a thousand years, and threw him into the pit and shut it and sealed it over him, so that he might not deceive the nations any longer, until the thousand years were ended. After that he must be released for a little while. (Rev. 20:1–3)

Revelation continues to explain that all believers from all time will have returned to the earth by this point and will reign with Christ for a thousand years on the earth (the millennium, Rev. 20:4–6).

At the end of the thousand years, Satan is let out "for a little while" and then ultimately defeated and thrown into the lake of fire and sulfur to be tormented day and night forever and ever (Rev. 20:7–10).

Next comes the unbeliever's judgment (the great white throne of judgment, Rev. 20:11–15).

And finally, the old heaven and old earth pass away and the new heaven and new earth that have been prepared for us will be brought down out of heaven from God (Rev. 21:1–2). Finally, God's dwelling place will be physically with us again, as it was in Eden. No more tears, pain, crying, or mourning (Rev. 21:5). All will be fully redeemed and restored.

Twelve Tribes of Israel and the New Jerusalem

When referring to the new Jerusalem made for the new earth, Revelation always clarifies it is "from God." "And I saw the holy city, new Jerusalem, coming down out of heaven *from God*" (Rev. 21:2, emphasis mine). I envision it like a project He's been working on. Jesus said, "In my Father's house are many rooms. If it were not so, would I have told you that I go to prepare a place for you? And if I go and prepare a place for you, I will come again and will take you to myself, that where I am you may be also" (John 14:2–3).

Revelation 21 describes the intricate ornamental work done to beautify the city of Jerusalem in the new heaven and new earth. A couple of verses stood out:

> It had a great, high wall, with twelve gates, and at the gates twelve angels, and on the gates the names of the twelve tribes of the sons of Israel were inscribed—on the east three gates, on the north three gates, on the south three gates, and on the west three gates. And the wall of the city had twelve foundations, and on them were the twelve names of the twelve apostles of the Lamb. (Rev. 21:12–14)

Did you notice there were twelve gates with names of the twelve tribes of Israel inscribed on them? The city honors the tribes or sons of Israel who led the people under the old covenant. Did you also notice the city has twelve foundations, and on them were the twelve names of the twelve apostles of the Lamb? That's the twelve apostles or disciples from the New Testament. Judas was replaced after he betrayed Christ. I think it's interesting that Revelation calls them the twelve apostles of the Lamb, as if to highlight their association with Christ in relaying His testimony and creating the church.

The Bible contains sixty-six books. The first thirty-nine books make up the Old Testament, and the last twenty-seven books make up the New Testament. Testament simply means "covenant." By calling the first thirty-nine books the "Old Testament," what is actually being said is they are the books that represent the old covenant before Christ came. The last twenty-seven books represent the coming of Christ and the new covenant He instituted with His death and resurrection. With this in mind we can better understand Revelation 21. The new Jerusalem will honor the twelve sons of Israel who led and instituted the people of God under the old covenant times, and the new Jerusalem will honor the twelve disciples who began the church and led her under the new covenant.

There was an era of time where people were teaching that the church replaced Israel. They would say anytime you see the word Israel in your Bible, replace it with the church and the promise applies. But that's not true. The church and Israel are distinct from each other throughout the Bible. Revelation confirms this by its description of the new Jerusalem memorializing both the twelve tribes of the sons of Israel and the twelve apostles of the Lamb separately yet together to make up the city.

There's something special about Jerusalem. Even back in Old Testament times, God chose the city of Jerusalem as the place where His name would rest (2 Chron. 12:13). My mother used to write my name on all of my school supplies, because when your name is on something, everyone knows it belongs to you. Revelation 22:4 says, "They will see His face, and His name will be on their foreheads." In the end He is going to make sure we and everyone else know that we are His. Yes, Jerusalem is His, but God also writes the names of the twelve tribes and twelve apostles of the Lamb on the city as if to say it's not just His, it's ours. We are the children of God—heirs of God and coheirs of Christ (Rom. 8:17).

"But Zion said, 'The Lord has forsaken me; my Lord has forgotten me.' [The Lord replied,] 'Can a woman forget her nursing child, that she should have no compassion on the son of her womb? Even these may forget, yet I will not forget you. Behold, I have engraved you on the palms of My hands; your walls are continually before Me'" (Isa. 49:14–16). The Lord has engraved us on the palms of His hands; we are His and He is ours. The verse says, "Your walls are continually before Me." I can just picture Him preparing the new Jerusalem up there in heaven and simultaneously penning these words through His prophet to the Jewish people. I can just see Him in that moment staring at the walls where He has written the names of the twelve tribes of the sons of Israel. "Your walls are continually before Me; I will not forget you. I'm preparing a city that is ours together. Your name is on it, and My name is on you. Even though your mother may forget you, I will not forget you."

Hebrews 11:8–10 says (italics mine),

> By faith Abraham obeyed when he was called to go out to a place that he was to receive as an inheritance. And he went out, not knowing where he was going. By faith he went to live in the land of promise, as in a foreign land, living in tents with Isaac and Jacob, heirs with him of the same promise. *For he was looking forward to the city that has foundations, whose designer and builder is God.*

Abraham was looking forward to the city that has foundations. What He didn't know was that the twelve foundations of that city had to have the names of the twelve apostles. Jesus had to come first. The city wasn't complete with only the names of the twelve *tribes* written on it. The church had to exist before that part of the city could be built with the names of the twelve *apostles*. Although given early, the promise was still true and firm. Abraham recognized that the city he was looking forward to had God as its designer and builder, just like Revelation 20–21 says. And he waited in faith.

Revelation shows us what we have to look forward to in that new city as we wait in faith:

And I saw no temple in the city, for its temple is the Lord God the Almighty and the Lamb. And the city has no need of sun or moon to shine on it, for the glory of God gives it light, and its lamp is the Lamb. By its light will the nations walk, and the kings of the earth will bring their glory into it, and its gates will never be shut by day—and there will be no night there. They will bring into it the glory and the honor of the nations. But nothing unclean will ever enter it, nor anyone who does what is detestable or false, but only those who are written in the Lamb's book of life.

Then the angel showed me the river of water of life, bright as crystal, flowing from the throne of God and of the Lamb through the middle of the street of the city; also, on either side of the river, the tree of life with its twelve kinds of fruit, yielding its fruit each month. The leaves of the tree were for the healing of the nations. No longer will there be anything accursed, but the throne of God and of the Lamb will be in it, and his servants will worship him. They will see his face and his name will be on their foreheads. And night will be no more. They will need no light of lamp or sun, for the Lord God will be their light, and they will reign forever and ever. (Rev. 21:22–22:5)

CHAPTER 11

Unveiling the End
(Joseph)

MY SEVEN-YEAR-OLD NEPHEW HAS a secret decoder light with an invisible ink marker. He ran to me one day and said, "Antler?"—yes, he calls me Antler—"Can I write on your hand with this?" And as any sucker of an aunt would say, I said, "Sure!" I couldn't see *what* he was writing because the ink was invisible, so when he was done, I said, "What's it say?" And he motioned for me to follow him to get the secret decoder light that would illuminate the invisible message written across my hand. He shined the light on it and then smiled bashfully from ear to ear as I read it. It said, "I love Antler." I exclaimed, "Aww! I love you too!" and scooped him up in a big hug.

The secret decoder light allowed me to see the message that could not be seen or felt with one of my five normal senses without the light. The message was there. It just wasn't natural for me to see it without the help of the light. Maybe there's some sixth sense out there in some creature that would be able to see it naturally, like those creatures who can see heat or see in the dark or something. We may never know. But the senses I have couldn't see the message without the decoder light. Sometimes Scripture is that way. The message is there but it's sort of disguised. We need the light of the Spirit to shine on the Word as we read so the more hidden messages are made clear to us.

Jesus disguised his messages to the masses by using parables, and sometimes even his own disciples needed help understanding or seeing the real meaning behind them. Likewise I believe God has disguised some end times messages within the stories of the Old Testament. We've seen some of those come to light through this book. This chapter will reveal more if the Spirit is willing to be the light to help us see.

The story of Joseph is the most fascinating story of them all to me because there are over one hundred points of analogy between Joseph and Jesus. We will barely skim the surface, but we are going to see some hidden treasures surface in the life of Joseph that bring deeper revelation of Christ and His plan.

Why are so many of the mysteries of God hidden throughout the Word? Why not lay them out plain and clear so *anyone* could see them, find them, and understand them? This is something Jesus's disciples wondered out loud as well, so we aren't alone in our questions. Matthew 13:10–17 recounts:

> Then the disciples came and said to him, "Why do you speak to them in parables?" And he answered them, "To you it has been given to know the secrets of the kingdom of heaven, but to them it has not been given. For to the one who has, more will be given, and he will have an abundance, but from the one who has not, even what he has will be taken away. This is why I speak to them in parables, because seeing they do not see, and hearing they do not hear, nor do they understand. Indeed, in their case the prophecy of Isaiah is fulfilled that says:
> 'You will indeed hear but never understand, and you will indeed see but never perceive. For this people's heart has grown dull, and with their ears they can barely hear, and their eyes have closed, lest they

should see with their eyes and hear with their ears and understand with their heart and turn, and I would heal them.'

But blessed are your eyes, for they see, and your ears, for they hear. For truly, I say to you, many prophets and righteous people longed to see what you see, and did not see it, and to hear what you hear, and did not hear it."

It seems there are some mysteries that are too precious and too dangerous in the hands of the wrong person. Some mysteries can only be entrusted to those who have the Holy Spirit giving them ears to hear and eyes to see.

My prayer is that He would give those of you desiring the deeper things of Christ ears to hear and eyes to see so your heart will see Christ in a new and more intimate way and become drenched in hope through the message. The amount of sovereignty and authority God has is comforting to me. It makes me realize I don't need to worry about a thing. All I have to do is focus on being faithful and connected to Him, and He will work out the rest.

I have a quote hanging on my mirror by Mother Teresa that says, "God does not demand that I be successful. God demands that I be faithful." The result is in the hands of God, good or seemingly bad. We are only responsible for being faithful to Him. When we remain faithful to God no matter what like Joseph did, everything falls into place at the proper orchestrated times. Even though we mess up and lose our faithfulness at times, He is sovereign enough to weave the lost time back into the plan. Don't lose heart when you stumble in the wrong direction. Just turn yourself around and get back on track without condemnation, and trust.

I was scrolling through Facebook one day and saw a post by Lisa Bevere that said, "If you think you've blown God's plan for your life, rest in this. You, my beautiful friend, are not that powerful."[49] I laughed out loud and loved it deeply all at the same time!

How many times have you gone to a place of darkness believing you've ruined everything and are a detriment to God and His plan? I say to you: You, my dear, are not *that* powerful. He's got it. Just turn around and get back on. You aren't responsible for the eternal results. He works those. You are only responsible for keeping your heart seeking Him day by day.

"On the last day of the feast, the great day, Jesus stood up and cried out, 'If anyone thirsts, let him come to Me and drink. Whoever believes in me, as the Scripture has said, "Out of his heart will flow rivers of living water"'" (John 7:37–38). Notice Jesus didn't say to come drink and believe and then *make* rivers of living water flow from your heart. Nope. He said come and drink and believe. Then the result that is beyond your power will be that rivers of living water will flow out of your heart. The results are not up to you. You are only responsible for being faithful to God and faithful to who you know He has called you to be.

You might be like me. I have a tendency to worry about everything and everyone around me, which can affect me and the plan negatively. When I worry about things, my understanding is not giving God enough power. The following verse makes my heart rest. "The king's heart is a stream of water in the hand of the Lord; he turns it wherever he will" (Prov. 21:1). The king—the most powerful man in a country—even his heart is turned here and there by the Lord. God allows that which He allows, so it may not always look divine, but rest assured he tells the circumstances and harmful people around us just like he told the oceans, "You can only come this far and no further." He is all-powerful—just waiting for the fullness of transgression to be completed so He can sort the wheat from the tares. Let it happen like He's letting it happen. Surrender is the best way. He will make all things right again. Your losses, your tears, your loneliness, your pain—it will all be wiped away in the end. Endure for the night and joy will come in the morning (Ps. 30:5).

Often the most thriving churches in the world are the churches under great persecution. When people of God are under hardship, suffering, or persecution, the Spirit of God will often come in the midst of it in the most intimate ways if we'll let Him. Then we get squeezed and we bleed more of the Spirit. And the Spirit is always producing and bringing life to what it touches. We find ourselves wanting an easy life of leisure. But if He gave us that all the time, we would be stagnant. When you've had all you can take, hold on just a little longer. What you need is right around the bend.

So how close *are* we to the rapture of the church and the second coming of Christ? Close, really close. In the book of Genesis, I believe Joseph is a picture of Jesus, and the narrative is a map outlining the end plan. Even though this book has touched on the lives of many men of faith, more real estate in Genesis is given to Joseph than any of the other patriarchs. Genesis 37–50 tells his story. That's thirteen chapters! It's almost as if the author is screaming to the reader: pay attention! If someone gets thirteen chapters in the inspired Word of God in Genesis, where that isn't typical, there's something to it. I'm going to highlight some of the Joseph-Jesus analogies for you. If you enjoy digging deeper into this kind of thing, get a book called *Gleanings in Genesis* by Arthur W. Pink. He's one of my favorites because he dissects passages and makes me think on a deeper level. God uses his books to open my eyes to deeper treasures, and I'm indebted to him and his book for confirming to me that I was on the right track when I began to doubt myself.

When we read the story of Joseph, it's hard not to see Jesus foreshadowed in it, and rightly so. Keep in mind Jesus was Jewish as you track the Joseph-Jesus analogies. Jesus's blood brothers are the *Jewish* people, not Gentiles. You're probably at least familiar with the story, so I'll hit the highlights.

> Joseph was *sent* by his father to his own brothers, but his own received him not. (Gen. 37:12)

Jesus was *sent* by His Father to His own brothers (the Jews), but His own received him not. (John 1:11)

Joseph was *stripped* of his robe, his robe of many colors. The robe was taken by the brothers before they threw him in a pit. (Gen. 37:23)

Jesus was given a robe and was *stripped* of his clothes, which were divided among men by casting lots at the foot of the cross. (Matt. 27:27–35)

Joseph was *sold* into slavery by his brothers for the average price of a slave at that time. (Gen. 37:28)

Jesus was *sold* by Judas for the price of a slave. (Matt. 26:14–15)

Joseph was *falsely accused* by Potiphar's wife and sent to prison. (Gen. 39:11–18)

Jesus was *falsely accused* by the Pharisees and sent to the cross. (Matt. 26:57–27:26)

Joseph was sent to jail and considered buried forever. (Gen. 39:19–20)

Jesus was crucified and considered gone forever. (Matt. 27:32–50)

Joseph was imprisoned between two men, the cupbearer and the baker who had committed offenses against the king. Joseph interpreted the dreams of both men and told the baker he would be executed, and he told the cupbearer he would be freed and restored to his place in the king's service. (Gen. 40)

Jesus hung on the cross between two thieves. Jesus revealed that one would go to eternal death and the other would be with Him in paradise. (Luke 23:32–43)

(Side Note about the cupbearer's and baker's dreams in the story of Joseph: It's interesting to note that the cupbearer's dream revealed a vine with branches that budded and grew clusters that ripened into grapes. He took the grapes and pressed them into Pharaoh's cup and placed them in Pharaoh's hand. The vine represents Jesus; the grapes, the blood of Jesus. The vine grew and produced grapes by no effort of the cupbearer. He simply received the grapes and squeezed them as an offering to Pharaoh. He was saved and restored to his place in the king's service, just as we who receive the blood of Christ as an offering to God are restored to the King's service through the blood.

The baker's dream, on the other hand, revealed his baked goods being given to Pharaoh, but birds kept eating it out of the basket on his head. The dream revealed that he would be executed by hanging on a tree and the birds would eat his flesh from him. This is a message about self-effort or trying to "earn" your way into salvation. We can be the best bakers, but our efforts get eaten by the birds before ever arriving to God. It's only when we trust in the power of the blood of Christ as our offering like the cupbearer that we can be saved. No amount of effort will be enough. We will be spinning our wheels trying to do enough, but the birds will be eating our baked goods all the while.)

Joseph *rose* up from the jail pit (where he was considered dead) to become the right-hand man of Pharaoh when he interpreted Pharaoh's dream with the power of God. (Gen. 41:14, 39–40)

Jesus *rose* from the grave to the right hand of the Father defeating His own death by the power of God. (Rom. 8:34)

After Joseph arose from the jail, he interpreted Pharaoh's dreams, revealing God's warning and future plan. (Gen. 41)

After **Jesus** arose from the grave, he appeared to John in a vision revealing God's warning and future plan contained in the book of Revelation. (Rev. 1:1)

Joseph rose to the right hand of Pharaoh, second in command, to oversee what was to come. (Gen. 41:39–40)

Today **Jesus** is seated at the right hand of the Father to oversee what is to come. (Matt. 22:44; 1 Peter 3:22)

The parallels are striking, aren't they? But that's not all. The interpretation God gave Joseph for Pharaoh's dreams revealed not only a message for his day but also a message for the end times. Prophecy often comes true on multiple occasions before it is complete. So let's look at the prophetic dream for both meanings.

The Egyptian Pharaoh's dream envisioned seven cows, attractive and plump. After seven attractive and plump cows came seven ugly and thin cows. The seven ugly and thin cows ate the seven attractive and plump cows. Pharaoh awoke and then went back to sleep and had a second dream. In the second dream there were seven ears of grain, plump and good. After the seven plump and good ears of grain came seven ears of grain that were thin and blighted by the east wind. The seven thin ears of grain swallowed up the seven plump ears of grain.

By the power of God, Joseph interpreted the dream. He explained that the two dreams were one. The doubling of the dream meant that it was fixed by God, Who would bring it about. The seven plump cows in the first dream and the seven plump ears of grain in the second dream were one and the same. They represented seven years of plenty and abundance. The seven thin cows in the first dream and the seven thin ears of grain in the second dream were one and the same. They represented seven years of famine.

Joseph explained that the seven years of famine would be very severe, so much so that all the years of plenty would be forgotten. So Joseph proposed a plan to Pharaoh that would help the country endure the coming famine, and because of his God-given wisdom, he was put in charge of that plan at Pharaoh's right hand. The time of plenty came, and then the time of severe famine came, just as Joseph had interpreted. Because Egypt was prepared for the famine when it came, it became the country that Israel went to once the famine was severe and they were out of food. Joseph's brothers, who had once sold him into slavery to Egypt, now came to him and bowed down before him and wept with him in repentance when they realized who he was. So what was God's reason for the severe famine? In *The Complete Bible Commentary*, George Williams drives this point home while alluding to the prophetic end-times significance of the dream (brackets mine to show the Joseph-Jesus analogies):

> This famine was designed by God, not only to bless and instruct Egypt, but mainly, to be the means of bringing Joseph's brothers in repentance to his feet. It is all, possibly, a picture of present and future facts. The true Joseph [Jesus] in His present rejection by His brethren [the Jewish people] takes to Himself an election from among the Gentiles. The completion of that election, if this picture may so be interpreted, will be followed by "the time of Jacob's trouble" [the Great Tribulation] the effect of which trouble will be to cause the Sons of Israel to recognize Him whom they had pierced, and to mourn and weep. (p. 39)[50]
>
> *Taken from* The Complete Bible Commentary © *Copyright 1994 by George Williams. Published in Grand Rapids, MI. Used by permission of the publisher. All rights reserved.*

Therefore the prophetic dream can also be seen as a picture of the reason the great tribulation must come in the end times—to turn the Jewish people to repentance so they will bow down before Jesus, finally recognizing Him whom they had pierced. Genesis mentions Joseph weeping over this situation many times. He exercised sternness, kindness, and goodness in the midst of the famine, which eventually led his brothers to repentance. His brothers wept before him when they finally saw him for who he was. The great tribulation will bring about the same result in the end times. It will be a severe event, but it's quite possibly the only way the hearts of Jesus's original brethren (the Jewish people) will turn to Him once and for all. What great lengths He goes to for His people!

When studying the numbers in the Bible, certain numbers consistently mean certain things. For more information on this, read *Number in Scripture: Its Supernatural Design and Spiritual Significance* by E.W. Bullinger. Seven is generally known as the number of completion or entirety. So when a prophetic dream or vision mentions the number seven, it might mean a literal seven for its first fulfillment, but for future fulfillments, the seven can mean completion or entirety.

Right now we are in a biblical era called "the age of the Gentiles" (see Luke 21:24; Rom. 11:25). Jesus came first as a Jew to the Jewish people, but when they rejected Him, He went to the Gentiles. Salvation among Gentiles exploded and has not stopped since. We are in the age of the Gentiles. Egypt, being a Gentile nation, is a picture of the Gentiles. God, with Jesus at His right hand, is reigning over the Gentiles, just as Pharaoh, with Joseph at his right hand, was reigning over Egypt. The seven years of plenty and abundance are the times we are currently in. The "harvest" of souls among Gentiles is plentiful and abundant during this era. Our time is now (2 Cor. 6:1–13). When the age of the Gentiles has reached its "completion" (the symbolism of the number seven in the dream), the tribulation is coming. The tribulation will go on until His purpose for it is "complete."

Just as Egypt was spared from feeling the severe effects of the famine, so will the Gentiles be spared from the severest parts of the tribulation thanks to the rapture of the church. Just as the famine brought the Jewish brethren to Joseph asking for bread, the tribulation will bring the Jewish brethren to Jesus asking for bread. Jesus, being the Bread of Life, will be able to satisfy the hunger of the Jewish people when they come to Him during that time. And when they realize who He is, they will weep and their hearts will fully turn to Him as never before. They will finally be committed and loyal out of deep, deep love that can only come out of the kind of darkness they will be saved out of through Christ's kindness and mercy.

God hasn't broken His covenant with His Jewish people. Anyone who teaches He has is mistaken. The New Testament book of Romans expounds upon this mystery in detail. As Joseph wailed and wept for his brothers, Jesus weeps for His original brothers, the Jewish people. In that day the prophecy of Isaiah will be seen:

> Comfort, comfort my people, says your God. Speak tenderly to Jerusalem, and cry to her that her warfare is ended, that her iniquity is pardoned, that she has received from the Lord's hand double for all her sins. . . . Go on up to a high mountain, O Zion, herald of good news; lift up your voice with strength, O Jerusalem, herald of good news; lift it up, fear not; say to the cities of Judah, "Behold your God!" Behold, the Lord God comes with might, and his arm rules for him; behold, his reward is with him, and his recompense before him. He will tend his flock like a shepherd; he will gather the lambs in his arms; he will carry them in his bosom, and gently lead those that are with young. (Isa. 40:1–2, 9–11)

Turn our hearts to You, O God. Draw the souls of both the Gentiles and the Jews during these last moments in history, and let us be a part of that kingdom work while we are still here on earth. We long for the completion of the family of God, for the curse of sin that causes us so much pain and heartache to be broken, and we long to be with You forever. Help us persevere, living lives worthy of the calling we have received. It's only because of Jesus, that we can stand before You with such assurance and hope. Unending love and praise for Jesus, our Redeemer, forever! Amen and amen.

Final Word from the Author

COMING UP WITH BOOK titles is hard. How does an author sum up so many pages of words in just a few small words? After finishing the rough draft of this book, I plopped down on the couch next to my husband feeling discontent with my title once again. I sat there flipping through a thesaurus, trying to come up with more word options. Finally, I got frustrated and said, "Justin, help! What am I going to name this book?" And he, in his quick wit, said, "Hmm, all I've come up with so far is *From the Lord to You, Bippity-Boppity-Boo*." As I was staring at him in shock about to burst into laughter, he added, "I mean, you can use that if you want. I'm still thinking though." He makes me laugh hard with his witty humor!

Had I chosen his title, you might not have ever picked up this book. Or maybe you would have? I'm really not sure at this point! But regardless, the fact that you stumbled upon this book and read it up until these last words means something to me. I'm thankful you entrusted your time to me and what I felt the Lord lead me to write for you. I don't take that lightly.

It has been fun journeying through Genesis together. Now that you see how closely the first book and the last book of the Bible tie together, will you take the time to read through the book of Revelation as a sort of postscript to this book on Genesis? I believe you'll find Revelation come to life for you. In fact the one who reads Revelation is actually blessed: "Blessed is the one who reads aloud the words of this prophecy, and blessed are those who hear, and who keep what is written in it, for the time is near" (Rev. 1:3). Give yourself the opportunity to be blessed by the Spirit by doing that.

What will you do with what has stirred in your heart through these pages? Do you feel the urgency of the end drawing nearer and nearer? Do you feel the call to a deeper walk with Christ—one that lives for eternal things over temporal things? So much of what people, even Christians, tend to live for won't matter in eternity. Let's commit together today to self-assess every month or two. Go ahead, stick a reminder on your calendar. When that reminder comes up, ask yourself, "Is my life currently more oriented toward goals and ambitions that will pass away or is it more oriented toward what's going to matter eternally?" Sometimes it takes keeping a vision for your life casted to keep it on the right track.

There's a verse I love that says, "We all, with unveiled faces, are looking as in a mirror at the glory of the Lord and are being transformed into the same image from glory to glory" (2 Cor. 3:18). From glory to glory—don't you love that? In other words, from God-moment to God-moment, we are being transformed. Over the course of a month or two, we should all have accumulated a good number of God-moments, each one transforming us more and more. Then you can then look back and see where God has brought you and look forward to where you see the momentum of those moments directing you.

If you look back over the past month or so and see that you're still in the same place you were the previous month, let that be a fire under you to make the necessary changes to focus on Him and all that matters for

FINAL WORD FROM THE AUTHOR

Him. There is a calling on your life, Believer. Go where He sends you. Crush the fear that's holding you down and step up into your calling in faith that it is He Who empowers you for every good work. Care far less about what you can get in this life and far more about what you're accumulating for the next life.

Though you may be persecuted, disliked, or encounter troubles on every side because of your life for the gospel, you cannot be destroyed until your work is done. Fight the good fight. Live the faith. Finish strong.

With you in Christ,
Lauren

Revelation 22:12–13

Behold, I am coming soon . . . I am the Alpha and Omega, the first and the last, the beginning and the end.

Endnotes

1. Wrath and Grace Facebook Page, accessed 15 May, 2018, https://www.facebook.com/wrathandgrace/posts/the-modern-church-is-producing-passionate-people-with-empty-heads-who-love-the-j/1880938285313662/.

2. For more information about various theories: Millard J. Erickson, *Christian Theology, 3rd ed.* (Grand Rapids: Baker Academic, 2013), 337–357.

3. E.W. Bullinger, *Number in Scripture: It's Supernatural Design and Spiritual Significance* (Midlothian: Alacrity Press, 2014), 14.

4. Bullinger, *Number in Scripture*, 12–14.

5. Arthur W. Pink, *Gleanings in Genesis* (Chicago: Moody Press, 1981), 53–54.

6. Brené Brown, "Quotes," *Goodreads*, accessed May 22, 2019, https://www.goodreads.com/quotes/838768-when-we-can-let-go-of-what-other-people-think.

7. Timothy J. Keller, Redeemer Presbyterian Church Sermon "Jesus, Our Priest," Gospel in Life and Redeemer Presbyterian Church, November 12, 1995, https://gospelinlife.com/downloads/jesus-our-priest-6415/.

8   Keller, "Jesus, Our Priest," https://gospelinlife.com/downloads/jesus-our-priest-6415/.

9   Arthur W. Pink, *Gleanings in Genesis* (Chicago: Moody Press, 1981), 66–67.

10 Thomas Purifoy, *Is Genesis History?* (Nashville: Compass Cinema, 2017), DVD.

11 J. Hampton Keathley, III, *The Judgments (Past, Present, and Future)*, accessed April 1, 2018, https://bible.org/article/judgments-past-present-and-future.

12 Charles Dickens, *A Tale of Two Cities* (Mineola: Dover Publications, 1998), 1.

13 George Williams, *The Complete Bible Commentary* (Grand Rapids, MI: Kregel Publications, 1994), 15–16. Used by permission of the publisher. All rights reserved.

14 Warren W. Wiersbe, *An Old Testament Study—Genesis 1–11: Be Basic, Believing the Simple Truth of God's Word* (Colorado Springs, CO: Cook Communications Ministries, 1998), 135. Used by permission of David C. Cook. May not be further reproduced. All rights reserved.

15 Arthur W. Pink, *Gleanings in Genesis* (Chicago: The Moody Bible Institute, 1922, 1950), 133.

16 George Williams, *The Complete Bible Commentary* (Grand Rapids, MI: Kregel Publications, 1994), 16. Used by permission of the publisher. All rights reserved.

17 Williams, *The Complete Bible* Commentary, 15. Used by permission of the publisher. All rights reserved.

18 Johann Hari, *The Likely Cause of Addiction Has Been Discovered, and It Is Not What You Think*, Huffpost, accessed April 15, 2018, http://m.huffpost.com/us/entry/6506936?ncid=fcbklnkushpmg00000063.

19 Hari, *Likely Cause of Addiction*.

20   Joel C. Rosenberg, "Modern Israel Turns 70—here are 70 fascinating facts about the modern Jewish State you might not know!," accessed April 23, 2018, https://flashtrafficblog.wordpress.com/2018/04/20/modern-israel-turns-70-here-are-70-fascinating-facts-about-the-modern-jewish-state-you-might-not-know/.

21   Peter W. Stoner, *Science Speaks* (Chicago: Moody Press, 1958), 97–110.

22   Josh McDowell and Sean McDowell, PhD, *Evidence that Demands a Verdict: Life-Changing Truth for a Skeptical World* (Nashville: Thomas Nelson, 2017), for further study.

23   Francis Thompson and adaptation by Brian and Sally Oxley, Sonya Peterson, and Dr. Devin Brown, *The Hound of Heaven: A Modern Adaptation* (Ft. Myers, FL: Emblem Media, 2014), 43.

24   Thompson, *The Hound of Heaven*, 68.

25   U.S. News & World Report, "Best Countries for Power," accessed May 28, 2019, https://www.usnews.com/news/best-countries/power-rankings.

26   Wikipedia, "List of Jewish Nobel Laureates," accessed April 18, 2018, https://en.wikipedia.org/wiki/List_of_Jewish_Nobel_laureates.

27   Pew Research Center, "Religious Landscape Study," accessed May 28, 2019, https://www.pewforum.org/religious-landscape-study/.

28   Arthur W. Pink, *Gleanings in Genesis* (Chicago: The Moody Bible Institute, 1922, 1950), 148.

29   Pink, *Gleanings*, 141, 152.

30   Warren W. Wiersbe, *NT Commentary—Luke 14–24: Be Courageous, Take Heart from Christ's Example* (Colorado Springs, CO: David C. Cook, 2010), 67–69. Used by permission of David C. Cook. May not be further reproduced. All rights reserved.

31   Keith E. Swartley, *Encountering the World of Islam* (Littleton: BottomLine Media, 2014), Lesson 2, God's Promise to Muslims, Kindle Edition.

32   Swartley, *Encountering*, Lesson 1, Muhammad's Youth, Kindle Edition.

33   Swartley, *Encountering*, Lesson 1, Prophet of Allah, Kindle Edition.

34   Swartley, *Encountering*, Lesson 1, Arabia in Muhammad's Time, Kindle Edition.

35   Swartley, *Encountering*, Lesson 1, Prophet of Allah, Kindle Edition.

36   Swartley, *Encountering*, Lesson 1, Interaction with Jews and Christians, Kindle Edition.

37   Swartley, *Encountering*, Lesson 8, When Did Corruption Occur?, Kindle Edition.

38   Bilquis Sheikh with Richard H. Schneider, *I Dared to Call Him Father: The True Story of a Woman Who Discovers What Happens When She Gives Herself to God Completely* (Old Tappan: Chosen Books, 1978), 116–117. Used by permission of Chosen Books, a division of Baker Publishing Group.

39   Sheikh, *I Dared to Call Him Father*, 117. Used by permission of Chosen Books, a division of Baker Publishing Group.

40   Keith E. Swartley, *Encountering the World of Islam* (Littleton: BottomLine Media, 2014), Lesson 1, Interaction with Jews and Christians, Kindle Edition.

41   Swartley, *Encountering*, Lesson 1, Interaction with Jews and Christians, Kindle Edition.

42   Easton's Bible Dictionary, "Machpelah," Matthew George Easton, accessed May 3, 2018, https://www.biblestudytools.com/dictionary/machpelah; The Jewish Virtual Library, "Hebron: Tomb of the Patriarchs (Ma'arat HaMachpelah)," accessed May 4, 2018, www.jewishvirtuallibrary.org/tomb-of-the-patriarchs-ma-arat-hamachpelah.

ENDNOTES

⁴³ *The MacArthur Study Bible,* ESV, "The Introduction to Obadiah," (Wheaton, IL: Crossway, 2010), 1257–1258. Used by permission of Thomas Nelson. www.thomasnelson.com

⁴⁴ Billy Graham, *The Holy Spirit: Activating God's Power in Your Life* (Nashville, TN: Thomas Nelson, 2000), 92. Used by permission of Thomas Nelson. www.thomasnelson.com

⁴⁵ Justine Cosman, "Five Important Benefits of Stretching," accessed May 24, 2018, www.wholebodyhealth-pt.com/wbhptblog/2017/2/20/the-amazing-benefits-of-stretching.

⁴⁶ Got Questions, "Why is God going to give us a white stone with a new name?" accessed May 23, 2018, https://www.google.com/amp/s/www.gotquestions.org/amp/white-stone-new-name.html.

⁴⁷ Arthur W. Pink, *Gleanings in Genesis* (Chicago: The Moody Bible Institute, 1922, 1950), 252.

⁴⁸ Bible Study Tools, "Jacob's Trouble and the Great Tribulation," accessed May 24, 2018, https://www.biblestudytools.com/commentaries/revelation/introduction/jacobs-trouble-and-the-great-tribulation.html#9798E.

⁴⁹ Lisa Bevere Facebook Page, accessed May 28, 2018, https://www.facebook.com/lisabevere.page/photos/a.284485715446/10157193824345447?type=3&sfns=mo.

⁵⁰ George Williams, *The Complete Bible Commentary* (Grand Rapids, MI: Kregel Publications, 1994), 39. Used by permission of the publisher. All rights reserved.

Bibliography

Bible Study Tools. "Jacob's Trouble and the Great Tribulation." Accessed May 24, 2018. https://www.biblestudytools.com/commentaries/revelation/introduction/jacobs-trouble-and-the-great-tribulation.html#9798E.

Brown, Brené. "Quotes." Goodreads. Accessed May 22, 2019. https://www.goodreads.com/quotes/838768-when-we-can-let-go-of-what-other-people-think.

Bullinger, E.W . *Number in Scripture: It's Supernatural Design and Spiritual Significance*. Midlothian: Alacrity Press, 2014.

Justine Cosman. "Five Important Benefits of Stretching." Accessed May 24, 2018. www.wholebodyhealth-pt.com/wbhptblog/2017/2/20/the-amazing-benefits-of-stretching.

Dickens, Charles. *A Tale of Two Cities*. (Mineola: Dover Publications, 1998).

Easton's Bible Dictionary. "Machpelah." Matthew George Easton. Accessed May 3, 2018. https://www.biblestudytools.com/dictionary/machpelah.

Erickson, Millard J. *Christian Theology, 3rd. ed.* (Grand Rapids: Baker Academic, 2013).

Got Questions. "Why is God going to give us a white stone with a new name?" Accessed May 23, 2018. https://www.google.com/amp/s/www.gotquestions.org/amp/white-stone-new-name.html.

Graham, Billy. *The Holy Spirit: Activating God's Power in Your Life.* (Nashville, TN: Thomas Nelson, 2000).

Hari, Johann. *The Likely Cause of Addiction Has Been Discovered, and It Is Not What You Think.* Huffpost. Accessed April 15, 2018. http://m.huffpost.com/us/entry/6506936?ncid=fcbklnkushpmg00000063.

Keathley, III, J. Hampton. *The Judgments – (Past, Present, and Future).* Accessed April 1, 2018. https://bible.org/article/judgments-past-present-and-future.

Keller, Timothy J. Redeemer Presbyterian Church Sermon. Gospel in Life and Redeemer Presbyterian Church. November 12, 1995. https://gospelinlife.com/downloads/jesus-our-priest-6415/.

Lisa Bevere Facebook Page. Accessed May 28, 2018. https://www.facebook.com/lisabevere.page/photos/a.284485715446/10157193824345447?type=3&sfns=mo.

MacArthur, John. *The MacArthur Study Bible*. ESV. "The Introduction to Obadiah." (Wheaton, IL: Crossway, 2010).

Pew Research Center. "Religious Landscape Study." Accessed May 28, 2019. https://www.pewforum.org/religious-landscape-study/.

Pink, Arthur W. *Gleanings in Genesis*. (Chicago: Moody Press, 1981).

Purifoy, Thomas. *Is Genesis History?*. Nashville: Compass Cinema, 2017. DVD.

Rosenberg, Joel C. "Modern Israel Turns 70—here are 70 fascinating facts about the modern Jewish State you might not know!" Accessed April 23, 2018. https://flashtrafficblog.wordpress.com/2018/04/20/modern-israel-turns-70-here-are-70-fascinating-facts-about-the-modern-jewish-state-you-might-not-know/.

Sheikh, Bilquis with Richard H. Schneider. *I Dared to Call Him Father: The true story of a woman who discovers what happens when she gives herself to God completely*. Old Tappan: Chosen Books, 1978.

Stoner, Peter W. *Science Speaks*. (Chicago: Moody Press, 1958).

Swartley, Keith E. *Encountering the World of Islam*. (Littleton: BottomLine Media, 2014). Kindle Edition.

The Jewish Virtual Library. "Hebron: Tomb of the Patriarchs (Ma'arat HaMachpelah)." Accessed May 4, 2018. www.jewishvirtuallibrary.org/tomb-of-the-patriarchs-ma-arat-hamachpelah.

Thompson, Francis and adaptation by Brian Oxley, Sally Oxley, Sonya Peterson, and Dr. Devin Brown. *The Hound of Heaven: A Modern Adaptation.* (Ft. Myers, FL: Emblem Media, 2014).

U.S. News & World Report. "Best Countries for Power." Accessed May 28, 2019. https://www.usnews.com/news/best-countries/power-rankings.

Wiersbe, Warren W. *An Old Testament Study—Genesis 1–11: Be Basic, Believing the Simple Truth of God's Word.* (Colorado Springs, CO: Cook Communications Ministries, 1998).

Wiersbe, Warren W. *NT Commentary—Luke 14–24: Be Courageous, Take Heart From Christ's Example.* (Colorado Springs, CO: David C. Cook, 2010).

Williams, George. *The Complete Bible Commentary.* (Grand Rapids, MI: Kregel Publications, 1994).

Wikipedia. "List of Jewish Nobel Laureates." Accessed April 18, 2018. https://en.wikipedia.org/wiki/List_of_Jewish_Nobel_laureates.

Wrath and Grace Facebook Page. Accessed May 15, 2018. https://www.facebook.com/wrathandgrace/posts/the-modern-church-is-producing-passionate-people-with-empty-heads-who-love-the-j/1880938285313662/.

Order Information

REDEMPTION PRESS

To order additional copies of this book, please visit www.redemption-press.com.
Also available on Amazon.com, BarnesandNoble.com, and www.laurenreeves.com.
Or by calling toll free 1-844-2REDEEM.

www.ingramcontent.com/pod-product-compliance
Lightning Source LLC
LaVergne TN
LVHW041632060526
838200LV00040B/1553